When
ANGELS
Make House Calls

Edited by
Ruth Rendely
& Angela Mailander

Seraphim Alliance

When Angels Make House Calls

Edited by Ruth Rendely & Angela Mailander

Copyright © 2018 Ruth Rendely

Published by Seraphim Alliance

First Edition
LCCN: 2018964831
Softcover ISBN: 978-1-4218-3819-9

Dedicated to

The Thirteen Seraphim who created the Blueprint

Table of Contents

Introduction

In the first days of the New Year I often become inspired with fresh ideas and plans for the coming year. I believe this process is true for many of us who feel the freshness, and worldwide pause that is associated with the shared Western celebration by half the world's population.

On the third day of 2017 I remember thinking that "Yes, I have written the two books that I intended to write in this lifetime—*Seraphim Blueprint: The Power of Angel Healing* (2007) and Y*our Multiple Souls: How they Direct Your Creativity, Genius, Complexity, and Moods* (2015)—but couldn't my skills as an author be used in less strenuous endeavours? Then I suddenly became inspired by a notion that has now become a reality. Why not have spiritual, short story contests, with results announced at the triennial Seraphim Blueprint Festivals? [The Seraphim Blueprint is an international organization that I founded with a Seraph, in 1995.] In 2017 we were holding a festival in late May, so there was plenty of time for entries to be submitted before the festival.

And voilà that is exactly what happened. Because I wanted us to start small, we limited the contest to Seraphim Blueprint practitioners. We still had plenty of entries most of which are published in this book. Of the fourteen stories included, twelve are by Teachers of Seraphim Blueprint. We also provided a cash prize for the First and Second winners of the contest, with almost all stories to be subsequently published in a collected volume of short stories which you are about to read. Our First Prize went to Masaru Yoshihara, of Tokyo, Japan, and our Second Prize went to Mary Hernandez, of Naples, Florida. Our intention for 2020 is to allow short story entries from the general public, and thus make this offering another way to advance our goals on the world stage. See the end of this book for details.

As an added bonus to our first volume, Andrew Ramer, co-author of Ask Your Angels, has agreed to include one of his poems "The Dream Gardener" as a foreword to this book.

Enjoy.

Ruth Rendely

Chairperson, Seraphim Blueprint

The Dream Gardener

By Andrew Ramer

The dream gardener plants dreams
in the dream garden.

Each morning he hoes the soil
and plants the small clear seeds in rows.
He waters them
and watches the new plants grow.
By noon the shoots are standing straight and tall.
By sunset the shimmering dream flowers
are fully grown and beginning to drift off
into the world,
each one carrying inside
another dream
for someone else to dream
that night.

The dream gardener
has been doing his work for years and years.
Your parents, your grandparents,
and their parents too,
dreamed dreams that he and his parents and grandparents

planted in his garden
at the far edge of the world.
But sometimes,
when he lies awake in bed,
listening to the sounds
that drift up into his garden
he is sad.
Because all the drifting flowers from his garden
look the same.
But some bring dreamers happy dreams,
and others carry nightmares instead.

One night
the frightening scream of a child
waking up from a nightmare,
perhaps it was you,
was so upsetting to the dream gardener
that he sat up in his bed,
turned on the light,
scared as if it had been

his own bad dream,
and said,

"From this time forward
I will never plant
another dream seed again."

Next morning the dream gardener got up
went out into the garden
and planted ordinary flower seeds,

big seeds and small ones,
but not a single dream seed.

That evening,
sitting comfortably on his porch
with a steaming cup of tea
and a plate of cookies
on the table in front of him
he was happy.
"No one will wake up
in the dark
afraid and crying,
calling out for their parents
ever again."

And that night,
snug in his cozy bed
he listened for sounds of crying
but there were none.
And he himself slept soundly, soundly, soundly
until the sun came up.

The next afternoon
he was trimming the hedges in his garden
when he noticed something curious
coming up the slopes
toward his garden.
It wasn't a sound,
it wasn't a smell,
it just a feeling,
a sense,

not that anything was wrong,
but that something
something wasn't right.

And the day after that,
the funny feeling
was stronger yet,
like the odor of something unpleasant
coming up over the hills,
cold and wet.
But the nights were quiet.
No one woke up scared,
and the dream gardener
in his bed,
slept happily for hours.

At the end of the week
the feeling
was stronger than ever.
And now it came with the sounds
of irritation
of upset,
and anger.
He could hear doors banging
down in the world,
hear pencils snapping
and someone's coffee mug
hurled across the room.
He put down the packet
of petunia seeds he was planting
to listen to the sound

of your mother,
turning to shake a finger at you,
her voice all cranky.

The crankiness continued.
Soon, it was all over the world,
the sounds of people getting nasty,
yelling at family and friends,
at other shoppers,
and even at their favorite store clerks.

"This is not good,"
the dream gardener said.
"Something is wrong in the world."
He heard Tommy,
teasing Griselda his cat.
And he heard Sarah
calling her little brother
"a selfish spoiled brat."

Although the sounds were upsetting
they came from far away.
Everything was peaceful in the dream garden
and the dream gardener spent his days
planting roses and lilies,
tulips and hyacinths,
and all the flowers
he'd never had time to plant before.

And that night in his bed,
the world was oh so quiet.

"I could come to like this,"
said the gardener,
as if he'd been put on
an ice cream and cookies diet.
Yes, the nights were still,
no nightmares – anywhere.
But each day was noisier than the one before it.
Down in the world
all he could hear were the sounds
of anger and shouting,
of anger and fear.

Soon horns were blasting,
and people were screaming at each other.
Fathers were fighting with their children,
and sisters and brothers
were hitting and yelling
and breaking each other's things.
All of those sounds
came echoing up into the dream garden,
its sacks of unplanted dream seeds,
sitting in burlap sacks
in a rickety old shed.
"Oh my, oh my,"
said the gardener,
"this is worse
than any nightmare."

That night was quiet,
and the gardener slept well again,
but he had to put cotton in his ears

when he worked in his fields.
But no cotton could silence
the booming
coming up from the world.

Just before dawn the next day
the gardener was awakened,
by such a thunderous noise
coming up from his garden.
And all at once he knew for certain
that all of the noise down in the world
began when he stopped planting dreams.
So he leaped out of bed
grabbed his shirt and pants,
jumped into them,
put on his socks and shoes,
and raced out into the garden,
his shoe laces loose.

As fast as he could
the gardener ran
to the little shed
at the edge of the trees
where he stored his unused dream seeds.
And the noises were louder
than they'd ever been before,
booming and yelling,
shouting and slamming.

With a sack over his shoulder
and a rake in one hand

he ran out to an unused plot of earth
turned the soil
and started planting.
Row after row he planted,
as fast as he could,
tossing hands full of clear dream seeds
into the dry brown earth.
Then he filled up his watering can
and marched up and down the rows
watering the seeds he planted,
happy to see the dry soil darkening.
And because they were dream seeds
they soon began to sprout,
but the noises from the world were so loud,
loud of screaming and shouting
that the gardener despaired
of what might happen
down there
in the world.

By noon
the dark green stalks were growing tall
and then tiny dream flowers began to emerge
at the ends of every stalk.
And by sunset,
the sky painted coral and gold
hundreds of dream flowers
were floating across the fields
sparkling, shimmering,
then they rose up into the sky
carrying dreams,

good dreams and bad dreams
up and out into the world.

Exhausted,
the dream gardener
collapsed into a chair.
He hardly slept at all that night,
listening.
Not sure if he could hear
any difference in the sounds
coming up to him
from the world.

But the next day
the world was quieter.
The gardener could tell.
And he planted new dream seeds
certain
that his work was making a difference.
And that night
just as he turned off his bedroom light
he could hear the cry of a little child
waking up from a bad dream.
And the dream gardener
fell asleep again.
Happy.
Knowing that we need good dreams to cheer us
and bad dreams to release
the upsets that we carry.
That if we don't have them
we feel worse and worse.

In a few days
the world was back to normal.
And the dream gardener
stopped one morning
at the edge of his fields
to enjoy all the sounds
that came up to him from the world.
Then he grabbed his rake
grabbed a sack of dream seeds
and began to plant them
as he does every day now
every day.

The End

A Simple Person

There seems to be something to spirituality, and there appears to be some people who can achieve outstanding success by knowing about it, and using it as a tool.

As a self-development magazine reporter, who was chasing success in various careers, I, a twenty-eight-year-old defeated dreamer, thought about spirituality often, especially when I was interviewing successful people.

I was born in Nikko, a rural area of Japan. Originally, I was not good at studying even though almost every one of my childhood friends was. I started high school without cramming for the stiff entrance examination. Rural high schools generally have incompetent students. With that rustic background, students who graduate high school end up working for low wages. If one finds a suitable mate, given that background, and can get married, that would be considered lucky. And if one then can also raise a child, then that would be counted as a good successful life.

When I was a sixteen-year-old who accepted his future reluctantly, I found, by chance, a book entitled *The Psychology of Winning* by Denis Waitley. Somehow, I purchased the book and read it diligently. For a 16-year-old boy who had no learning ability or experience, it was almost the first time in my life that I finished reading a book without pictures, and with just typed letters. Like other non-academic 16-year-old boys at that time, I was only interested in reading comic books and porn.

The book said, "Change your life by yourself." These were unfamiliar words because I thought that life was decided by inherited circumstances and would be impossible to change. Am I able to change my life by myself?

Since I am a simple person, I challenged myself to change my life. I decided to become a newscaster working for a broadcasting station. I wanted to be a person who could encourage people by speaking. I had loved to talk since childhood and felt proud of it. So, first, I studied hard because a bachelor's degree was required to take the test for employment at a broadcasting station. And, somehow, I passed the university entrance examination that had previously seemed impossible with my meagre academic record.

The year I graduated university and started looking for a job was one of the hardest years for job-seekers. No male newscasters had been hired by any major broadcasting station nationwide. So, my dream did not come true.

I had dreamed my dream, tried to change my life, and failed. I was stupid! I felt so at the time. I had to find another company to work for. After some difficulty, I managed to get a job as a magazine editor.

"GOOD JOB, GOOD LIFE." That was company policy. How ironic! Even more ironic was the fact that I was assigned to be a self-development magazine reporter. I dreamed of success in life, but failed while telling about the ways others had made their dreams come true.

While creating magazine content, I was fortunate to

every day meet many famous, successful entrepreneurs. But even after interviewing them and listening to their success stories, I still could not grasp a way to make my own life a success. That was doubly ironic.

Seraphim Blueprint

Since I had almost no knowledge of spiritual things, or healing modalities at the time, it was mysterious to me that, during my experience of conversing with some interviewees, who were successful in a profession that seemed to have nothing to do with spiritual fields, would sometimes let slip phrases like "the law of attraction" or they would use words like "vibration" (high frequency), as if these words stood for a secret, cryptic phenomenon which should not be discussed with the public.

To succeed, do we need help from some spiritual force that is invisible, as most people who are successful claim? This is an unfamiliar idea for most ordinary people. I was amazed at such a ridiculous idea, and yet at the same time, if it were true, it seemed a glimpse into the secrets of this world.

While I was researching spiritual events on the internet, I found Seraphim Blueprint. The concept of receiving healing energy from the highest among sacred angels sounded weird from a common-sense point of view. And I was afraid that losers like me would not deserve to receive such sublime energy.

I applied to attend the workshop, still holding some fear. When I arrived at the workshop venue, I was relieved to see that there weren't any signs indicating that it was a cult group.

During the workshop, we received invisible healing energy through a kind of meditation that they called an "initiation." As the initiation began, I felt as if static electricity was running throughout my whole body. Also, at times, I felt invisible fingers pressing strongly on my forehead. That was a strange, but amazing experience.

In the middle of the workshop, during a discussion time, the teacher said, "I cannot recommend doing it frequently, but you can get answers from the Seraph by asking him something."

As I was scheduled to receive a courier delivery on that day, I asked in my mind, "Seraph, if you really exist, please let me know what time the courier will arrive today?"

And in my mind the answer came: 20:48. I saw the number clearly, with a pale light, like a neon sign.

This was the first time in my life that I'd had such an experience. So I thought I was going crazy. At the same time, I also thought with childish curiosity how wonderful it would be if the courier actually arrived at 20:48. It would be real evidence that there is a Seraph. If that happened, then I had channeled the Seraph!

On the other hand, I felt apprehensive. If the courier didn't arrive at 20:48, I'd feel stupid for believing in angels. I would then be forced to think that the Seraphim Blueprint workshops were a fraud, and I'd just lost ¥20, 000 (about $200), which was the workshop fee. In that case, I would be one of the miserable people who believe in unscientific things, such as angels, and who pay a lot of money for illusions. For me, at that time, paying 20,000 yen in one day was a big expense.

But then the workshop ended successfully, and, suddenly,

all the participants decided to go out to dinner together.

An aside here: With the advent of the Internet, spiritual energy work has become more common than ever and thus there is less need to hide if you believe in or do some kind of energy work. But there still is a risk that you might get cut off from friends and family. You also might lose an opportunity for promotion at your workplace. It is like being gay and living in a society that does not understand diversity. As it is, spiritual-minded people are still in the minority and are not yet understood.

That first night after the workshop was so pleasant for each participant because we could meet with a few similarly-minded people. Just a dinner party, but, as no one expected it to, it turned into a party, and we spent the next three hours together.

When I got back to my house after transferring trains, it was past 9:00 PM, and there was a delivery absence notice in my mailbox. The delivery time was stated on the notice as: 20:48.

I instantly believed in the existence of angels (since I am a simple person).

A Professional Healer

I went to Australia's Blue Mountains to visit Ruth Rendely, the lady who heads the "Seraphim Blueprint," and, on December 31, 2008, I got certified for teaching Seraphim Blueprint Levels 1 and 2. Returning to Sydney on the train that night, I attended the New Year's Eve countdown event among many strangers at Sydney Habour. As the New Year approached, I saw Sydney's New Year's Eve Fireworks display from an open area. It was so spectacular! I took the fireworks as blessings for me as a Teacher of the Seraphim Blueprint (since I am a simple person).

To tell the truth, I was a bit worried because, at that time, there was a rule that we had to teach Levels 1 and 2 to more than ten people to become a Teacher of Level 3 and higher. (That rule has since been revised.) I was worried that I wouldn't be able to find people who would attend a workshop with a loser like me.

But…laugh and grow fat, fortune comes in at the merry gate. Incredibly, I was able to gather twelve students in a workshop held shortly after returning to Japan. I had incurred a large debt with my round-trip ticket to Australia and the teacher-training course fee. Thanks to many students who gathered, however, I was able to repay the debt immediately in full. Nor did I have to focus on any advertising. Instead, after a little while, I became acquainted with a woman interested in spirituality. When the conversation turned to the topic of the Seraphim Blueprint, I mentioned that I had become a teacher of Seraphim Blueprint; she said, "Is it okay to hold a workshop just for me? If you think it would be more convenient, I will invite my friends." And she did gather eleven of her friends! Perhaps she was a guardian angel (of course she was also a living human being) who would lead me to a higher stage as a person or a healer? With that first class, I easily and instantly fulfilled the requirement for becoming certified to teach Level 3 and above.

Starting with that class, I found that I could earn many times more revenue from teaching healing classes than working for my former company, and I could do it without even advertising for this new business. It seemed as if people who showed up to study with me were like dogs on a hunt (kind of a rude example) sniffing after me until they found me. Unlike my own experience of finding the Seraphim Blueprint, I felt that their taking a Seraphim Blueprint workshop was somehow a necessary process for them (I don't know why), so I just helped them to follow their fate (which they had selected themselves).

I got so much confidence with that success, that I quit my company at the age of thirty, and decided to become a full-time healer and teacher (since I am a simple person).

Even with such independence as a full-time healer, I never have to think about earning money to eat for even one moment. If you are doing what you should be doing, then getting money to live is easier to grab than you can imagine (this can be clearly understood by those who have taken the Seraphim Blueprint Seraphic Tour of the Galaxy Course). And concentrating on the way of healing with a heart that is not captivated by greed, you attract more clients, which only leads to further monetary wealth and to the achievement and the reputation of being a healer.

While working as a healer, I am also healing and improving myself in every way, every day! Of course, I repeatedly use Seraphim Blueprint's energy initiations, and every time you use them, you will find something new about the energy and about yourself. Finally, I became able to experience the positive aspects of life, and now I can enjoy the benefits of this world in many ways. Every time I find something wonderful in this world, I experience some brand-new thing that makes me stronger, healthier, wiser, and (hopefully) more handsome.

The Once Defeated Dream Came True!

And it was not long before I was forty years old, and the path of newscaster, that I had broken away from, and given up wishing for a long time ago, opened up to me again. A man appeared who can only be described as a guardian angel (and of course a living human being too) who led me to the next stage of my development as a newscaster. He had many strong connections to the broadcasting industry, and powerfully promoted me as a newscaster. Even though I had no experience and would normally be considered too old to start this professional career, I was appointed as the newscaster, or radio personality, of a broadcasting program.

Surprisingly, when I work as a news commentator, or radio personality, my skills cultivated as a healer for the past nearly ten years has helped me so much more than I ever thought it could. First, through facilitating healing workshops, I am using similar skills to what a newscaster does during radio programming. And when I talk to an unknown number of people as a radio personality, people with different beliefs and belief systems, it has become natural not to use prohibited terms or discriminatory expressions. I can entertain them without using speech that makes anyone uncomfortable. The experiences of being in contact with people who are mentally injured, or those who are very sensitive from time-to-time have made me more capable as a broadcaster.

In addition to the Seraphim energy, my encounters with wealthy people, not only in terms of money, but in every way, has changed me. If I had kept working for a company reluctantly, as I used to, I would not have had the opportunity to meet such wonderful people. These experiences have transformed me from being an ignorant and reckless loser into a person who can empower, heal, and help others to shine.

I don't feel a desire to boast of my success with any feeling of looking down at others or wallowing in a sense of superiority. I just do what I can do. I'm satisfied with what I am doing. When I was only thinking about success in my youth, I couldn't achieve any success at all. I couldn't manifest any of my dreams. Now I think it was probably the universe's way of teaching me that "It's no use trying in that way." At that time, I felt a very strong feeling of resentment against the whole world, but now I am grateful for that experience as a kind of preparation for what was to come.

These days, I do not care if my (egoistic) dreams come true or not. I think that it is enough if I can do what I can to convince myself and gain something indispensable for living, such as money and human relationships. When I began to think in that way, my dreams came true continuously, almost as if it were just fun and in spite of my age, while ordinary folk believed that it is too late for me to make dreams come true. It is ironical.

I don't want you, the reader, to be offended by my showing off my own success (I think that my success is closer to a miracle, rather than just success).

Also, not all people who take Seraphim Blueprint courses and become Teachers will be guaranteed to follow what appears to be my destiny (Some people may feel that they do not want to embody my way of living here).

Nevertheless, if you dare to follow what I have preached about Seraphim Blueprint, the existence of an angel, my encounters with his energy—all these changed me from being a foolish, selfish person to someone whom others appreciate.

Whether an angel changed me, or I changed myself through the energy of an angel, I don't know. I don't care, (since I am a simple person).

However, if I had not met Seraphim Blueprint teaching, I would not be who I am today. I can say that with certainty.

Well, what would you like to experience with Seraphim Blueprint?

* * *

Masaru Yoshihara was born 1978 in Nikko, Japan (a world heritage site). After graduating from Waseda University Faculty of Law, he worked in a government-affiliated financial institution for four years before becoming an editor of a career development magazine. In 2009 he became a full-time healer and Teacher of the Seraphim Blueprint.

My Mother's Reincarnation

Two prophetic dreams foretold my mother's death. In the first, we are alone together when she suddenly turned to me, and all I saw was her moon-shaped face smiling beatifically and saying, "Ruthie, I love you so much." I awoke (immediately) and realized that she had never (in real life) expressed such a direct emotion to me, and I relished every wonderful feeling that the dream evoked. I was living in Tokyo, thousands of miles away from my parents, who were in Florida, but I told some close friends how this was the most direct experience of my mother's love that I'd ever had.

Then, a few weeks later, the second dream occurred: My mother and I were part of a group of tourists traveling by train in Hawaii. Never mind that Hawaii has no trains. The train occasionally stopped for the group to disembark and see the sights, and then, at an appointed time, we were to board the train again. The first time we disembarked, my mother was walking so slowly that I had to encourage her to keep up with me so we wouldn't be late for the train's departure. We barely made it. At the second stop, her slow walking caused the same problem, and this time, she made almost no effort to get back on the train, as I rushed to board, she was left behind. Later, I learned that trains in dream language represent life's journey. Not getting back on the train was a sign that life would continue without her.

Two weeks later my sister called from America to say that Mother was dying of melanoma, a type of skin cancer, and the doctors had given her three weeks to live. This information had come with no warning, as my mother had hidden an earlier bout of melanoma from my sister and me, telling us it was a benign skin cancer. I immediately made plans to fly to Florida to be with my parents and deal with this shocking revelation.

After a 21-hour flight from Tokyo, I saw my mother in the hospital. I noted her deep tan and no loss of bodily fat, making her look healthier than we were told she was. Because I was in deep denial about her impending death, I kept trying ways to reverse everything. Before leaving Japan, I had contacted two psychic healers there to work on her, and after I arrived in Florida I contacted a Hawaiian Kahuna who chose to work on my mom after she saw "What a big heart she has." I was so grateful hearing these words, and it made me think of all the times that my mother expressed and acted upon her concern for humanity, over her own small needs. I inherited that quality from her. While I was running a Non-smoker's rights group in Iowa, she was actively involved in a Non-smoker's rights group in Florida, unbeknownst to me. She was also on a crusade to change the official name of 'catfish' to something more palatable (double entendre) as she said this humble fish needed a PR makeover, as it was cheap and so good for you, but people shunned it because of its name.

When we first met in the hospital, she was concerned about my completing the doctorate in history and inquired about that. I said that I would hear from my doctoral committee soon about their opinion of my latest version of my dissertation. As I was her only unmarried daughter, she was also concerned about that, but I reassured her that I was in a very loving relationship with a caring Japanese businessman.

The doctors at the hospital had completed their round of chemo and radiation on my mother and told us we could care for her at home. My sister, Marsha, felt that, given my arrival, she could return to Maryland to be with her family and resume her regular work. I agreed that this was fine, and that I would gladly take over the care of my mother with the help of my father. This was the end of the first week of December 1986, and the holiday celebrations became just an unnecessary irritant in the daunting task we faced.

Once my mother was at home, I tried to put on a brave face in front of her and slowly decided to keep a strict routine in caring for her. We did not employ a nurse, and my father and I took on all the chores of feeding her, helping her shower, and go to the bathroom. I set meals at the same time daily and attempted to get her to exercise her feet to keep her circulation going. I frequently asked her if she was experiencing any pain, and she always answered "No."

I can't recall that, during the next few weeks, she ever initiated a conversation. She would respond to our queries, but in the simplest, shortest way, with a flat response lacking any emotion. I couldn't even tell if she was depressed, although she had accepted the doctor's opinion of her condition. When my mother was alone with my father, I could hear the two of them arguing—about what I didn't know. My father's emotional state was fragile, of course, and this resulted in angry outbursts, which were often directed at me. I supposed this was because I was closest at hand. When this became unbearable, I threatened to go back to Tokyo and leave him alone with her. Then he would apologize and become calmer again.

After three weeks of caring for her and being emotionally and physically drained, I allowed my aunt Charlotte, my mother's sister who lived nearby, to visit and give me some relief. We decided to see "Crocodile Dundee" at a local theatre. The film was so amusing that, for two hours, I forgot the overriding events and truly laughed for the first time in months. It was not only a relief; it was also my first introduction to things Australian.

It is often said that people who are getting ready to transition often hold out for certain family members to appear, or for certain holiday events to occur. This was the case in my mother's transition. My sister had been gone three weeks, but returned on January 1st, 1987. And my Aunt Charlotte came again to join us for a holiday dinner. While we were eating in the dining room, my mother made her final transition. When I went to check on her after the meal, I couldn't tell if she was still alive. Her body was warm, but I couldn't see her breathing. I quietly called my sister into the bedroom to see if she could tell. She couldn't either. I decided that, maybe, the Hawaiian Kahuna who lived 3,000 miles away in California could tell us! When she answered the phone, she said that yes, my mother had passed. It was only then that I called my Father to tell him the sad news. When he saw his wife lying there, he kept repeating: "What a wonderful woman she was!"

At that point, I became extremely weak and couldn't take the next necessary steps. My sister, however, who had just arrived with fresh energy, took it upon herself to start the process that we hadn't prepared for. My mother had wanted to donate her whole body to a medical school, but had made no further preparation to do so. Because it was New Year's Eve, nothing was open, so we had to go with plan B, which was to have her cremated. My sister took care of all the details, and planned to hold a funeral service for the extended family a few days later in a large park. It was well attended by family members and a few of my parents' friends. I couldn't fathom how my sister was able to control her emotions and speak about our mother. I was silent for this occasion.

Then I started the process of returning to my life in Tokyo. As I flew over America on my return home, I kept begging my mother's soul not to let the plane crash just because she wanted me to be with her. I considered my mother to be my closest family member until then, and was extremely shocked that she passed so young, and before my dad, because it was he who had suffered from severe Tuberculosis, resulting in his hospitalization for six months; in addition, he was a 40-year smoker who only quit in his early sixties. Dad lived to be 88.

Nineteen eighty-seven was one of the most depressing years of my life on many counts, including my mother's death which had set up the year on its first day. I spent most of that year looking for different ways to recover from such a big and unexpected loss, a year which also included the end of my doctoral studies without receiving my doctorate, and the end of my "wonderful" relationship with my Japanese boyfriend. But we do know that a young Phoenix rises out of the ashes, don't we?

The one single thing that helped me to recover most was becoming a member of a small English school based in Yeovil, Somerset England that provided me with various paraphernalia to revive my interest in life. One of these tools was a pendulum, traditionally used as a psychic tool, but in my introduction to its benefits, I was told to strictly adhere to the health information it provided me via my own internal nervous system's wisdom. I spent about six months perfecting the use of this tool and, at the end of that time; I could correctly predict the weather about 24 hours in advance. In those days, before computer modelling of the weather, that was better than official forecasting.

I was not one to follow rules, however, so after playing with the pendulum for over half a year, I started getting more creative in asking questions of my nervous system. I never thought of myself as being particularly psychic, but when I started to ask questions about my own past lives and got some specific answers, I became more confident in my ability to use the pendulum as a psychic tool. Many people are probably clairsentient, as that is the kind of energy a pendulum picks up, but they don't know it because nobody has ever given them a pendulum, and most people are too scared of psychic gifts anyway to ever start out this way. And I have to seriously warn the reader not to play with Ouija boards, as they appear to hook directly into the lower astral realm where all kinds of disgusting beings live. One can be permanently damaged by such associations, and exorcisms are not pleasant experiences.

Somehow, however, while playing with the pendulum in

those early years, I was supremely protected. I chalked it up to long years of meditating; at that time, I had been a teacher of Transcendental Meditation for over thirteen years.

Thus, my psychic explorations began in earnest. One tool that the English esoteric school had given us was a kind of energy mandala with light blue cardstock movable parts. It was composed of a larger circle and a smaller circle; there were 21 numbers on the outer circle indicating a person's health. One could then take any photo of an individual and place it face down in the center of the circle and, touching the energy mandala with one hand, while swinging a pendulum with the other, one could determine the physical health of anyone on the planet.

While I didn't think that my mother would reincarnate quickly, and it could be many years until she did so, I was frequently testing the possibility that she had reincarnated by using this energy mandala with her photograph. You see that of the 21 numbers on the outer edge of the mandala, zero indicated perfect health and 21 indicated deceased. So about once a week I tested my mother's photo on the Mandala scale. And without fail she came up dead every time until the early part of 1988, when, suddenly, there was a change. She no longer registered under 21, but started to register under the zero point! I was dumbfounded! Could she have reincarnated?

Before this experience, I had asked questions about other deceased relatives, especially my maternal grandfather whom I adored. Grandpa Abe was so silent in his ways and such a religious Jew that I considered him a saint. When he died at 74, I wasn't thinking about him reincarnating, but with my newfound psychic abilities, I started asking such questions. I was told that he had been reborn in Cannes, France. Although Cannes is known for its film festival, I had no idea where it was in France. I looked at a map and found that it was a beachside resort on the Mediterranean. Well, one might say so what? But in my grandfather's case, it was the perfect location, because, while in his previous body as Abe, he always managed to live within walking distance of a beach. He loved the ocean and insisted on renting facilities near it when I knew him. So that impression seemed quite real.

It has been sometimes mentioned that retired people like to travel the world because they are shopping for a new place to live in their next lifetime. In the case of my parents, my mother spent the last ten years of her life traveling the world with my father, but there was one continent she went to that he had no interest in visiting. Thus, she travelled alone to South America and climbed Machu Picchu, later raving about how special it was at her age to climb to 8,000 feet above sea level. My mother did have a special interest in Latin America. When she was a young woman, she travelled to Cuba to visit some distant cousins there and studied Spanish because she'd so enjoyed her stay there. Even in the last three weeks of her life, I remember waking her from sleep early one morning to keep our rigid routine, and, as she was waking, she blurted out: "Oompah-pah! Oompah-pah!" She was imitating the sound of some musical instrument she was hearing in her dream that involved participating in a big street parade. I was so sorry that I had awakened her from such a happy dream.

So, on the day that the Energy Mandala indicated to me that my mother had begun the reincarnation process, I quickly asked where was she on the planet? I was told she was in Uruguay near the Argentinian border. This made so much sense to me. I quickly asked when I could see her and was told in twenty-four years! What?! Why so long? I then answered my own question when I began to realize how this made complete sense in the real world. For me to think of interacting with her in any way, she would need to understand what reincarnation is. And that would likely be beyond her childhood years. I also needed to learn to speak Spanish, or so I thought.

So it was 24 years in 2012, and I had begun making plans to seek her out. I began buying Spanish language CDs and listening intently whenever I heard Spanish spoken. I picked up some phrases slowly over time, and noted how my high school French studies helped in the process of learning such a similar language. I also was quite happy when, in 1994, I made a new friend whose home was in Argentina. I now knew someone locally whom I could consult about such a strange trip. I had always recalled how, in Paramansa Yogananda's book *Autobiography of a Yogi*, Yogananda reported the ways he located a reincarnated disciple of his own master, Shri Yukteswar, when, in his normal travels around India, he would raise his hands high using them as antennas facing in all directions to pick up the vibrations of this young disciple who had died of an illness at age eight. I decided that, once I landed in Argentina, I would use my psychic skills to help me pick the general area of my mother's residence, and then once I found the nearest town, I would walk around using my arms in the same way Yogananda once did.

But by 2012, the 24th year after my mother's death had come and gone, and I had yet to make this trip with such a special purpose. The pull to do so has waned over the years, and I have become satisfied looking into my mother's eyes in a wonderful black and white photo I have of her sitting beside my desk.

* * *

Ruth Rendely was blessed in 1994 with meeting a Seraph, of the Seraphim, who asked her to partner with him to bring out an ancient healing system that had been dormant since Atlantean times. She joined him to resurrect this method and founded the Seraphim Blueprint. Her first book *Seraphim Blueprint: The Power of Angel Healing* (2007) has been translated into Japanese, German and Turkish. Before 1989 Ruth had been a university history lecturer in both the United States and Japan

The Wings of Change

I am back. Again. Whenever I am inside the Hagia Sophia, I experience an incredible flow of inspiration; this place is, for me, a conductor of clarity. Pieces of internal wisdom, almost forgotten memories, life experiences and fragments of visions merge with universal insights like pieces of a giant puzzle that start to fall into the right place to reveal parts of a larger picture.

How did it all begin? Prior to 2005, I had no idea who or what Seraphim are. This suddenly changed, when I, seemingly by accident, stumbled into a workshop related to this topic. That day triggered a deep fascination with this subject, and sparked my strong desire to learn more about it. Ultimately, it motivated me to embark on an almost Indiana-Jones-like quest around the globe, trying to find evidence and traces of these high angels in religious teachings and ancient art and to uncover some of the mysteries of the Seraphim to understand their meaning and relevance for me today.

Almost everywhere I went, only few people know about Seraphim. I devised a quick survey as a conversation starter regarding this topic. It goes like this: Please point to one of the following six pictures that shows an image you associate with the word "Seraphim". The first photo is of a high-speed train flying through the countryside; the second one showcases a sparkling blue gemstone; the third portrays a bizarre fish swimming through a primordial ocean; the fourth depicts an angel with six wings in a piece of ancient art, the fifth illustrates an exotic flower; and the last one is a picture of a fabric with a distinctive pattern.

This quiz leaves many people scratching their heads even among the more spiritual crowds at holistic Expos where I give presentations. I think, if someone would have put me on the spot like this years ago, I probably would have picked the image of the exotic flower.

Things shifted significantly after a long chain of synchronicities had drawn my attention repeatedly to the exceptional Seraphim depictions inside the Hagia Sophia. It was a subtle, but very distinct guidance that expressed itself in a series of serendipitous events. The culmination point was my decision to embark on my first trip to Istanbul in 2012. I have returned here often since then, but I still remember clearly the unique mix of almost overwhelming emotions and sensory stimulation during the initial visit. Over time, it set into motion a process that deepened my understanding of the seraphic consciousness and the human perception thereof and it changed the trajectory of my entire life.

I am standing inside the Hagia Sophia, as I have many times before. Experiencing the dimensions of this building is humbling. Four gigantic Seraphim depictions adorn the ceiling. Their wings are reaching up to the edge from where the enormous dome arises. I love to position myself directly at the midpoint below. Being surrounded by these massive six-winged angels triggers something deep inside me.

Every visit here feels different. The Hagia-Sophia-experience has become a mandatory part of every one of my trips to Istanbul. But it is not only about the strong vibration of the location or the impressive accumulation of historic artifacts. There is a sense of importance and significance permeating this extraordinary building that draws me toward it again and again. My physical presence here always coincides with entering an altered state of mind and emotion which allows me glimpses of higher levels of truth and consciousness, and there is a strong sensation of connectedness. I also feel an immediate impact physically, a tingling sensation dancing through my body.

The Hagia Sophia is a true architectural wonder. It was the largest enclosed space on Earth when it was opened in 537 after only 5 years of construction and it maintained this status for over one thousand years. The name Hagia Sophia translates into "Holy Wisdom". It has been attracting travelers, explorers, and seekers from all over the world; it inspired writers and painters and still does. And it sustained its mysterious allure over the centuries, as is evident in that the Hagia Sophia is still the most visited historical monument in Turkey to this day. And I feel that, somehow, the enigmatic Seraphim depictions add to the almost magnetic force that attracts observers.

Suddenly, a group of four women and two men arrives, and they are positioning themselves right next to me. As they look around, their attention gets immediately captured by the four great winged beings who dominate the ceiling. The British tourists (judging by the accent) start debating what it is that they are seeing high above. "Are they angels? They look like angels. No, not really, they don't seem to have bodies... Are these wings? Wings??? And why so many wings? Six wings, really!?"

Oh yes, the topic of the wings…these questions are familiar to me. How I struggled with this concept some years back! When I was a child, it somehow seemed perfectly agreeable to my imagination that angels existed and that they had wings. But at some point, my critical thinking started to take over and my need to analyze and to understand changed this completely. I probably spent hundreds of hours on the topic of angels' wings. And now, today, this really does not even feel like such a big question any more. Interesting, how things sometimes shift. For me it happens, when I "can get out of my head," so to speak. When establishing a heart connection, things appear different; priorities change. It almost makes me laugh today, when I recall my long internal battles about this topic.

It seemed – for me at least - like an inherent contradiction that an angel, who is a non-physical entity, would have wings with feathers. A bird needs them to create force for lift-off. By flapping down, the wings generate high pressure underneath them, and that can push the weight of the bird's physical body up and off the ground. The wings are also necessary to provide the thrust for moving the bird through the air. How about the functions of the feathers? Generally, birds have primary and secondary feathers. The primary feathers, mostly ten on each wing, are essential for flying. If they are damaged, no take-off is possible. The secondary feathers are sustaining the bird in the air and giving it sufficient lift. All the feathers together provide a lightweight surface for pushing against the air. They are indispensable tools to control the nuances of the downwards and upwards thrusts and to maneuver into the desired directions.

If angels have no physical body, what do they need the

wings for? What weight do they have to lift, what resistance or opposing force do they have to overcome? Could an etheric being not just move by will or through mere intention? Ultimately, I was unable to reconcile these concepts. I even had several sleepless nights trying to find answers that seemed so fundamentally important to me back then.

Gone were the childhood days when the idea of angels seemed fascinating, and I loved the thought of having such invisible protectors and guides. Justifying the purpose of their wings had become almost an obsession. It developed into the central focus point on which my entire belief system seemed to depend. Whether to believe angels exist or to ban them into the realm of fairy tales for children—it all hinged on the wings for me…

The discussion among the visitors next to me continues. It is impossible for me not to overhear it. They keep sharing their ideas about the winged creatures and their possible meaning. It makes me smile when I listened to some of their comments alternating between a sense of wonder, curiosity and skepticism. As I am gazing at the Seraphim on the ceiling, some of the wing-theories come into my mind again. Should I share my thoughts with the group of debating strangers?

I could tell them about the theory that what appears to us as wings may not be designed for flying at all, but they might be shields of protection. It is interesting that the angels of lower realms are thought to have only two wings, but the angels who are at the top of hierarchy and who are residing at the highest vibrational levels are depicted with more wings: the cherubim have four and the seraphim have six. The Seraphim are defined as a group of high angels directly surrounding God, or, in other terms, they occupy the level

of consciousness closest to the Source. Based on this understanding, these shields might be necessary to protect the
angels from this constant blast of energy emanating from
the source of all that is. It is an etheric concept, equivalent to
how the Earth's magnetic field creates a protection from the
perpetual solar wind.

The Biblical interpretation of the wings of the Seraphim
is that they are used for veiling the angels' faces and to cover
themselves as an act of humility while they are in the presence
of God. They wish to express their modesty and loyalty by
preventing their own light from shining too brightly, so that
they will not be perceived as competing with the glory of
God. Maybe the shielding also goes both ways. Being so close
to the source of energy might bear a risk of assimilation or
melting back into source. To be able to sustain their individ-
uality, they might need a separating buffer. In addition, the
shields might also ward off unwanted energetic inferences
during the angelic travels, and protect us, our human bodies
and energy systems, when we interact with them. Do the depictions of the Seraphim not look like they are intentionally
withholding the full force of their light and are only allowed
to come through to the extent that we can handle it?

Maybe it would inspire the puzzled observers besides
me to hear the theory that the wings might serve as tools
to change direction and to navigate space, like setting sails
or using a rudder for steering a boat. Or, for me as a fan of
"Stargate SG1", I could compare it with programming the
correct destination coordinates before dialing out. When
observing birds fly on a windy day, I sometimes notice how
strong gusts can suddenly toss them around and how they
use their wings to regain control. Maybe there is such a

thing as "etheric weather" with energy blasts and frequency streams, and the angels use their wings to maneuver around obstacles and stay the course. Another aspect is the possible use of the wings as breaks to be able to slow down from lightning fast travels through space and time at a precise end point. Whenever there is a change of direction or a switch from the state of rest into motion and vice versa, the wings might facilitate these changes.

Looking at wings that way, it is very interesting to point out, that each one of the four Seraphim angels inside the Hagia Sophia has a distinctly different wing position. In most other places where I have encountered multiple Seraphim depictions next to each other, each image normally is just an identical repetition of the same Seraph. But here, for some reason, that is not the case. Is this an indication how they adapt to different situations to facilitate the optimal dynamic? A hidden message?

Synchronistically, one of the ladies next to me just pointed out to the others that each one of the angels was looking unique, and she speculated that maybe the various positions of the wings might signify different stages of their flight. I have to control myself and suppress laughing out loud. What is going on here? Telepathy? I continue to wonder if I should introduce myself to the group. Each one of them is very engaged in their conversation about angel wings.

Part of me would love to share the theory that maybe they are wings of transformation. It might be true that the angels, when dwelling in their natural "home-environment", are purely etheric and wingless indeed. But when angels interact with humans, they might choose to descend into lower realms that we humans also can perceive. In situations like that they might have to transform their entire being to maneuver these foreign territories. Creating an intermediate space, establishing some common ground between two different forms of existence, where we can interact with the Seraphim, might require as much, or possibly even significantly more of a change to the Seraphic consciousness than it does for us.

We humans can use a variety of techniques to expand our sensory awareness and consciousness. In turn, the Seraphim might use certain methods depending on the requirements of specific circumstances, and the use of wing-tools could be one of them. Accounts of interactions with angels that did not have wings seem to indicate that either the angels have the option and ability to switch the wings on and off, or the sensory awareness or state of consciousness of the witnesses fluctuated.

Spirit itself may need some substance to become tangible or visible in three-dimensional, physical reality. One idea is that water vapor might be the optimal medium to enable angelic beings to appear to us. If the angels were to use such vapors to aid in their appearance in denser realms, they might no longer be truly non-physical and weightless. The water might add enough mass to truly require wings to maneuver around. Is it a coincidence that freezing water droplets manifest as snowflakes with "six wings"? And isn't it interesting that freezing water vapor on a window crystalizes in fascinating feather-like ice flower creations?

I find myself thinking about several other theories, like the one that each wing is a multidimensional energy vortex; or the idea that there may be an evolution of spirit itself that is represented by the number of wings. The core thought is that every time a soul or spirit ascends, or, better, transcends one level of existence, it receives a pair of wings. Part of me really wants to share all these thoughts with the group of British ponderers. But I do not. The whole topic of angels with six wings is a rather confusing one, even for many people who have studied the hierarchy of angels. But then again, the entire concept of the existence of winged etheric beings requires faith: six wings, four wings or just two wings...

All these theories are just that: theories. I have also reconciled with the possibility that the wings have no purpose at all. Perhaps we are misguided by our human desire and need to understand, which then leads to the assumption of a purpose in everything. The whole topic of angels remains in the realm of mysticism. Much cannot be revealed in words because we are missing proper associations. But, of course, we cannot help but to ponder about it. Maybe having wings is simply something like a fashion statement: perhaps having six wings is an equivalent of wearing an Armani suit. Maybe angels like the way it looks and feels, and they get enjoyment from it.

We can easily overthink matters. I know!!! Our mind goes into overdrive and prevents us from perceiving the essence. All this information might just feed the inner critic. The need to understand can be a self-sabotaging act to distract us from the truly meaningful. I hope the British seekers get beyond the whole wing topic and focus on the core questions: Who are the Seraphim? What is their essence? What is their significance for us today?

Inspired art is a "mystical mirror" of the divine within; it resonates with the soul wisdom and can help us to find the keys to access deep inner knowledge and truth. It contains a lot of symbolism. And symbols can be a spiritual trigger for the observer. The more we focus on them, the more personal meanings will be discovered. Spiritual images empower our imagination. I trust the six British people were inspired by the artwork itself. They absorbed the images for a long time; they engaged thoroughly. Opening ourselves through this sense of wonder and curiosity creates space and opportunity for revelations. I didn't even have to share my thoughts with the puzzled observers next to me. I can trust that they will have divine guidance.

Suddenly, the group break off. Everyone seems to be going their own ways to explore other points of interest in this huge museum. One of the ladies turns around and asks me if I could take a photo. Preferably, she wants to have one of the Seraphim in the photo right above her. "I really like that one". She points to her favorite of the four. I smile. And I just respond, "Sure, aren't these angels amazing?" She nods and adds: "They are so mysterious".

I have to get down on one knee to get the perfect angle to capture the chosen Seraph right above the lady's shoulder. I do it gladly. I take a few photos, just to make sure. She says: "I love the angels! These seem to be very special ones". I nod in agreement and say, "Yes, they are magnificent." I hand her back her phone; she checks the photos and gives me an approving smile. I wish her a nice time in Istanbul and she fades into the crowd.

It feels to me like this lady certainly established a real connection with the Seraphim through her sense of genuine curiosity and wonder. The photo will be a good reminder. I think she intuitively realized that the Seraphim can be in- terpreted as the personification or the embodiment of the energy of divine love and that they are powerful spiritual intelligences we can communicate with. And maybe, she created a lasting bond and, after her return home, her favorite Seraph might make a house call at her place in the UK.

I bring back my focus to the angels and continue to open myself to the mysteries of the Seraphim.

* * *

Alex Brandin is a spiritual seeker, workshop facilitator, and writer. He primarily offers "Seraphim Blueprint" workshops in the US, Turkey, Japan, Germany and Switzerland. Originally from Germany, Alex currently resides in San Francisco.

Grandparents

What is it about grandfathers and grandmothers that is so enticing that their presence remains with us life-long, even ages after they have exchanged this life for a different dimension? This bond, this deep connection, how to explain it? Not that we usually spend much time with them at all: some vacations with them because our parents are traveling or because mother has to work?

But Papa Richard was special. My grandfather, Papa Richard Bodequin lived with us because my mother was a widow. He died when I had just turned six. Until then, he took care of me. My "boterham met confituur," as he would say in Dutch, "My sandwich with homemade preserves" was waiting for me every day after school, neatly cut into two symmetrical pieces, carefully laid out to the left and the right of my cup of "lait Russe," Russian Milk, which was a fancy name for a cup of warm milk with a drop of coffee, a tiny nebula which swirled and dissolved while I was chewing the sandwich. This image is burned into my brain bank as a silent token, a commemorative image of his unconditional love.

We got up together in the morning around six o'clock, the same time I still wake up every day, even after only five hours of sleep. We stood there in our tiny kitchen, built as an extension of the dining room, as most traditional town houses in Europe were configured. A closet, a sink, a Remy Martin gas stove to boil the water. Light came from the narrow inner courtyard ("cour") which stretched alongside the kitchen. At the end of this "cour" a wooden gate opened into the garden—not that there was much of a garden. It was a tiny piece of land, alongside Papa Richard's "atelier," his workshop, where he built beautiful furniture. That was his craft. Papa Richard was a furniture maker and a musician. We grew—and indeed it was "we," Papa Richard and I who took care of this precious little stretch of land that connected our house to an alley between the buildings—we grew and carefully watched our tomatoes. We watered the tobacco plants and harvested them to dry upside down, carefully attached to wires on the wall above the rabbit cage in his workshop. We gathered food for our rabbits on daily foraging excursions.

To this day, I recognize "our" wild medicinal plants also growing here in the meadows of California, on the other side of my Belgian childhood world: young clover, tender green of buttercup leaves, sorrel, nasturtium, dandelion, water cress from the creek...

Then there is the complex world of sounds and smells, like those Marcel Proust most famously evoked in his "À la Recherché du temps perdu": the smell of coffee; the lovely, yet harmful, smell of Cuban cigars. Smells to bring me right back to the Bergstraat (Mountain Street) #68, Oudenaarde, my hometown until I turned 18 and left for the University of Ghent never to return, except for occasional visits.

"Papa, why do you put a little bit of coffee in your cup,

then a tiny bit of sugar, then cognac and then more coffee?"

"Well my child, because otherwise the sugar will not dissolve, and the coffee would taste bitter."

Years later, I suddenly stopped next to an older man standing in front of a store window on Elk Avenue in Crested Butte, Colorado, to tell him, out of the blue: "Oh my, you are smoking a Cuban cigar. This reminds me so of my grandfather in Belgium." Startled, the man turned to me and mumbled, utterly amazed: "This is the nicest thing anybody has said to me in a long time. Usually, people turn away, or make nasty gestures as if I were poisoning them, or they make very rude comments." While I happily inhaled to enjoy this long-lost odor, a sudden smile brightened his face. He shook his head in disbelief and continued to look at me, as if I'd come from a different planet. As I continued my errand, I heard his happy comment: "Woman, you made my day."

In our living room, Papa gave private lessons in percussion to aspiring musicians. I sat on the stairs, watched the young boys and listened. I wanted to be a drummer girl, but "Girls play violin, not drums." I was very annoyed with the boys who could not master the correct rhythm, because I could repeat the cadenza exactly, silently drumming the fingers of both hands on my knees. My older brother Adrien, who clearly inherited Papa Richard's musical skill, received the training and soon joined the local Orchestra with Papa Richard.

Papa Richard played with the Philharmonic Orchestra in Oudenaarde. He took me to weekly rehearsals and Concerts, performed at a kiosk in the middle of the market place. Those lovely Art Nouveau structures served as a podium for musicians and the conductor; they were a staple of every little town in Belgium, as the concert halls are today. The orchestra was seated in the open, under a high copula, sustained by thin iron columns, elegant capitals, and delicate borders, all decorated with flowery plants, visible to the audience, but not protected from cold weather.

Every Sunday at noon, after High Mass, from May through September, the Orchestra offered free concerts to the public. Papa was Principal Percussionist, responsible for large and small drums, xylophones, bells, and the whole family of percussion instruments. The program mainly consisted of overtures from operas or symphonic compositions. Each concert would last about an hour, enough time for people to sit leisurely at terraces of cafés and restaurants around the plaza to savor their coffee or beer. And of course, standing room for everyone, because the "Grand Place" of my childhood was not a public parking place. Cars were very rare after the Second War, in the late forties and fifties.

Today, we sit in Davis Symphony Hall in San Francisco, in anticipation of Verdi's Requiem, his operatic master piece. As soon as the orchestra plays the "Overture", I am back on the plaza of my childhood; Michael Tilson Thomas no longer conducts the orchestra. He is replaced by Octave Simuys, the impressive conductor impeccably dressed in a black evening suit, standing at the kiosk of my childhood, his back turned to the audience, waving his arms, shaking his wild grey mane, holding a commanding baton in the air to make silence an integral part of the musical movements. Yes, the power of built-in silence to underline a hesitation, a subtle change in meaning, a shifting mood, and keep the audience enthralled, captivated, longing for the next notes and for the melody to finally exhale.

Sitting in a concert hall or listening to the classical radio station, I am surprised by the size of the musical repertoire preserved in my brain. A couple of opening bars and the melody unfolds in my head. I could hum along, but mostly delight in the power of impeccable memory with which the amazing instrument of our brain is gifted.

And then there was Papa Richard's daily evening ritual before I went to sleep: a sign of the cross with his thumb on my forehead: "God bless you and keep you"; a safety sign for the little girl afraid to leave the warm harbor of her bed to embark on the scary ocean of sleep for the night's journey.

In my living-room today, I maintain a little altar with candles in front of the photos of my dearest deceased family members. My mother, Blanche, a perpetual image of the "Mater Dolorosa," the Mother of Sorrow, staring at you, exhausted and bewildered, dressed in a black, a widow at age 36 with 4 small children. There is also my father Bernard, his green eyes intense and penetrating, a man whom I never knew and who was "the love of her life," in his leather bomber jacket, just months before his death, killed by the Nazis, at age 36. Their wedding photo: a very distinguished couple, Bernard impeccably dressed in dark suit with a bowler hat; Mama Blanche in a lovely dark satin coat and a cloche hat. Both wore white leather gloves, conforming to the etiquette of the thirties. There is also Papa Richard Bodequin on his wedding day to Maria Biassino, the grandmother who died tragically before my birth. The parents of my father, Bonpapa Florent Bral and Bonne-Maman Stephanie Vandenheule, are there toasting each other with a glass of wine at their Golden Jubilee Celebration. And last, there is a tender photo of Stephanie with her first-born in a white baptism gown, my father Bernard. I honor them with candles and mementos, carefully assembled over the years, discovered at antique stores, second-hands stores, or flee-markets, but selected from memory: a redwood level with a glass bubble in a copper fitting for Papa Richard; a mysterious old flat-iron for Bonne-Mama

They are my very beloved ones. I greet them every day and am grateful they gave me life!

* * *

Rita M. Bral, BA, MA, graduated from the University of Gent, Belgium Currently she is V.P. Corporate Communications of Software Research, Inc. From 1988-2002 she was Executive Director of Software Research Institute. Rita held the mandate of Honorary Consul of Belgium for Northern California and Nevada, from 1993-2013. In recognition of her services to the Belgian government, HRH Albert II awarded her with the titles of "Knight of the Crown" and "Knight of Léopold". Currently she serves on the boards of Education Francophone Bay Area and The Institute for European Studies at U.C. Berkeley.

A Typical Morning

I wake up at 6:00 as always. After washing my face, I call the Seraph.

"San...!" (Seraph's Name)

The Seraph appears with dazzling light. The Seraph looks both male and female. So I don't really know whether to use *he* or *she*, but I'll settle on *he*. He has a silver light body with six wings. The shape of the body is like that of a human being. He has a head, but he doesn't have eyes, nose, or mouth. His face is shining light.

I then say a few words out loud: "Vo..., attunement of the heart-center".

A sphere of white light with a diameter of about three meters appears around my body. Then the sphere shrinks toward the center of my heart. As it shrinks, the sphere's light becomes stronger. When the size of the light sphere becomes the same as that of my heart, the sphere starts rotating in various directions while merging its light energy with that of my heart. When the merging finishes, the attunement is done.

Next, I invoke "Iu..., healing of the weather." My spirit goes to the god of weather. He dwells in a golden shrine built on a white cloud. As I arrive in front of the shrine, He appears in front of me. He has the appearance of an old man, like a legendary wizard with a white beard, white robe, and a wooden staff.

I say, "Good morning, Master. Please let today's weather be comfortable."

The god, who looks like an old man, replies, "Granted" with a smile.

I say, "Thank you for today, too!" I also tell him, "I have a present for you, today."

And he replies, "What?"

Then I imagine some presents for him. A denim jacket and a colorful feather decoration appears. "Please put on these items," I tell him.

He says, "What are these?"

"This jacket is a trendy, cool outer garment that the young people of Earth really like. And this feather decoration is popular among shamans on Earth. How do they suit you?"

He puts on the jacket and feather decoration. "Hmmm, not bad. Thank you." He leaves with a smile.

The weather on that day was very pleasant with a clear sky.

The next day, when I chant "Iu…, please let today's weather be comfortable," the god of weather comes out wearing the denim jacket and the feather decoration attached to his head. I was quite surprised that he appeared wearing the gifts I had given him.

He tells me while touching his long, white beard, "It's good, don't you think?"

"Of course. It suits you. So cool!"

"Thank you. Hahaha…" He leaves with a smile. It seems that he liked the gifts I'd brought him.

Next, I chant "Em…; I purify and activate all of my cells."
The Seraph replies, "Done."

Three shining light disks of a meter in diameter appear above my head.

The bottom light disk slowly comes down. When it reaches my head, my brain cells begin to emit light and are activated one cell at a time. Dirt and impurities drop away and disappear like smoke. As the first disk of light reaches my toes, the second disk of light begins to come down. The second and third disks of light also purify and activate the cells of my whole body in the same way. My mind is cleared and I feel that my body is lightened.

"Thank you, Seraph."

"You are welcome."

Next, I invoke "Ip…; Please do the healing of my connection to Gaia."

A seraph with six wings appears and says, "Granted."

I become able to see countless light particles around me, countless particles of light gathered to me, and a tree of light grows up through my body. The tree of light spreads out branches more than fifty meters long, and each branch absorbs light particles and gathers the light to the thick trunk of the tree of light. Then, the light tree spreads its roots to the center of the Earth.

Several roots are growing fast and form a spiral through the ground. When the roots reach the center of the Earth, light energy is sent to the Earth's core. Following that, the energy of the Earth is sent from the Earth's core to me through the roots. An energy exchange is performed between me and Gaia, and the connection between me and Gaia is strengthened.

"Thank you, Gaia." I whisper.

Then an incarnation of Gaia appears. Her shape looks human, but her outer surface looks like some kind of silver metal. She wears no clothes and has a head, but no face. She has no hair, but the silhouette looks like a goddess.

"You are welcome," She says. Then the incarnation disappears into the ground.

Next, I invoke "Iu…; I heal the connection with the fairies and the devas around me."

A huge translucent sphere with a diameter of about one mile appears around me. Next, the inside of the sphere becomes dim. Other people inside the sphere are walking without noticing any special change. Then, a moon appears in the sphere above me. A goddess always appears with the moon, and the moon illuminates the surroundings with a soft and gentle light. Various elementals and fairies appear one after another—fire elementals, water elementals, wind elementals, Earth elementals, tiny salamanders, white sylphs, water fairies, and dwarves, as well as many other types of fairies. Fire fairies come up from a sunny place and from dwellings that have a kitchen with a stove. Flame fairies are burning and quivering like a candle's flame. Wind fairies emanate from the air. They move so quickly that they could hardly be seen. Where they had been, the wind is swirling and blowing. Water fairies come up from the river, or from canals along the roads. They change into various shapes. Sometimes they look like water droplets; sometimes they look like fish. When they gather together into a large river, they look like a water snake or dragon.

The Earth elementals and dwarves come up from the ground. They are cheerful and chatty, and they are also hard workers. They rarely appear in front of humans during the daytime. They feel uncomfortable in strong sunlight; instead, they prefer to play in the light of the moon. The spirits of the four major elements and the fairies of the four major elements come out of the ground and enjoy the moonlight.

I say, "Thank you very much for showing me your appearance, Spirits of the Four Elements and Fairies of the Four Elements."

They reply, "You are welcome! Thank you for the moonlight energy."

The fire fairies say, "When you want to burn something, call us anytime."

The wind fairies quickly say, "When you want to know something, ask us anytime."

The water fairies, looking like little girls, whisper gently, "When you want to wash away something, please call us anytime. We will wash away anything."

Earth fairies say, "When you want to connect strongly with the Earth, call us anytime. And if you pray, we will give you wealth."

When I look up to the sky, the Goddess of the Moon is shining very gently.   I tell the Goddess with a loud voice "I appreciate this gentle and rich light of the moon!"

Then the goddess spreads both hands with a smile and brings the light of the gentle moon further to the ground.

After thoroughly enjoying and appreciating these experiences, my consciousness returns to normal. Although these experiences seem to pass in a flash, they actually take a long time, but the surrounding time interlude flows by as usual.

Next, I invoke "Vo…; I activate Kundalini. I open the *Ida* channel. Then I open the *Sushumna* channel a minute later.

Then I open the *Pingala* channel after another minute."

A small golden dragon appears in my sacrum. And it goes up my spine in a clockwise spiral. A second small, golden dragon appears in my sacrum and it goes straight up my spine. A third small, golden dragon appears in my sacrum and goes up my spine, drawing a counter-clockwise spiral. The three small golden dragons activate my chakras one by one. The root chakra glows and releases energy. And then it rotates slowly. The chakras gradually open from the bottom to the top. And all the chakras open and are activated. All the chakras are connected by light and light flows through the chakra circuit from the crown chakra to the root chakra.

I see the Seraph's appearance clearer, and the Seraph's voice becomes plainly heard.

"Thank you very much, Seraph," I say.

"You are welcome," the Seraph replies.

Next, I chant the invocation, "Em...; Healing harmony with the expanding universe."

I close my eyes.

My consciousness floats in the air and rises.

My body is getting smaller and smaller.

I look down from over a mile up in the sky. My consciousness continues to move away from the ground. I can see the entire city where I live. The river looks slendor, and over there I can see mountains. I can see the coastline; I can see the shape of the prefecture where I live.

My consciousness rises still higher. And as I go up, the form of my consciousness grows even larger. The whole shape of Japan gradually becomes visible. However, my consciousness does not stop and it continues to rise. My consciousness escalates to such an extent that I can see all of

Asia. Horizontal lines in the surroundings draw round arcs.

My consciousness continues to rise further, and the size of my awareness also grows. At last the whole Earth becomes a sphere. My consciousness grows bigger still, as I can hold the Earth with both hands. My consciousness expands away from Earth.

I am aware of the moon. My perception becomes integrated with the moon. And then my consciousness passes through the moon.

Next I am aware of Venus. My awareness becomes integrated with Venus. Venus is similar in size to Earth. Although the surface of the planet has a stormy landscape, I feel the existence of life-forms. Then my consciousness goes through Venus.

Next I am conscious of Mercury. My consciousness becomes integrated with Mercury. I feel a very fast movement on Mercury. Then my awareness goes through Mercury.

Next I am conscious of the Sun. My consciousness becomes integrated with the Sun. When integrated with the sun, I feel warmth. The inside of the sun is a world of light and high temperatures. However, I feel life forms in the sun. They have a different form than the life forms humans can imagine, and they exist in a dimension different from the one human beings can perceive. There is a will of pure service that penetrates the solar system. And then my consciousness goes through the Sun.

Next I am conscious of Mars. My consciousness becomes integrated with Mars. It is a planet about the size of Earth. On this planet, the will to fight is high-lighted. And then my consciousness goes through Mars.

Next I am conscious of Jupiter. My consciousness

becomes integrated with Jupiter. That planet is hundreds of times larger than Earth. Jupiter is a planet of strong gravity and storminess. Then my consciousness goes through Jupiter.

Next I am conscious of Saturn. My consciousness becomes integrated with Saturn. That planet is silent with blue-gray energy. I cannot see anything in dimensions that human beings can observe, but it certainly feels like there is the existence of winged life-forms. And then my consciousness goes through Saturn.

Next I become conscious of Uranus. My consciousness becomes integrated with Uranus. That planet governs unpredictable fate. An old man wearing a purple robe who always monitors the planet appears there. And then my consciousness goes through Uranus.

Next I am cognizant of Neptune. My awareness becomes integrated with Neptune. The planet is always covered with a cobalt blue surface. And when integrated with this planet, one's forehead will be activated. I dive deeper and deeper into its ocean. The blue energy, like the deep sea, makes the imagination clearer. When integrating with Neptune, transformational energy to see what we normally cannot see is given to me. And then my consciousness goes through the Neptune.

Next I am conscious of Pluto. My consciousness becomes integrated with Pluto's. The planet is black and small, covered with a mysterious veil. There are few life forms. Instead, there is a desolate atmosphere, but it seems like there is something like a huge gate there. And then my consciousness goes through Pluto.

Next I am conscious of another planet in the solar system.

My awareness becomes integrated with that planet. I do not know the name of the planet. The planet is similar in size to Earth. However, the ocean cannot be seen, it has a dark overall color, and its appearance is different from the Earth's. When integrated with this planet, it looks quite different from the Earth, but it feels nostalgic. I feel the existence of a very advanced civilization on that planet. I feel a strange sensation that we do not know the existence of this planet even though the planet has been there for tens of thousands of years. I meet the main sentient being of that planet several times. And then my consciousness goes through the planet.

My awareness then spreads beyond the solar system. The solar system looks smaller and smaller, and the surrounding stars pass through me.

Then I am presented with a planetary system consisting of six planets. There is a blue-colored planet in the system. On this planet, there are mountains and oceans as on Earth, and it is richly vibrant with natural features. There are animal ecosystems, birds flying in the sky, and fish swimming in the seas. On the plains, where the mountains open, there are scattered communities where people live. Unlike Earth, the big cities have no skyscrapers or huge buildings. However, civilization is not impeded, but rather it seems that ecological balance has progressed ahead of the Earth's. The beings there have an advanced civilization with evolved consciousness, so that the planet is at peace and not polluted. And then my consciousness goes through that planet.

Next I pass beyond that planet. Then I reach a planet with a military civilization. There are many spaceships which are mechanized warships standing on the planet. The crews are lined up in order, and almost all the crews are armed. The civilization seems to be controlled by the energy of domination and commandments. There is no feeling of pleasure or joy there, but the residents of the planet do not seem to feel pain. My consciousness passes through that planet quickly.

Next, I reach another solar system consisting of three planets. One of them is covered with water. That planet has a civilization of aquatic life. Residents of the planet are swimming underwater mainly in the form of dolphins and whales. They have few tools and no machines. However, they have a high degree of civilization and high intelligence and are a much more evolved life-form than Earthlings. And my consciousness goes through the planet.

My awareness continues to expand. The stars look like tens of millions of grains of sand. And, finally, the whole image of the Milky Way spiral comes into view.

Still my consciousness continues to expand. The galaxy that looked so huge gradually becomes smaller. Then the neighboring galaxy appears slowly. Then the surrounding five galaxies appear slowly.

Still my consciousness continues to expand.

One hundred galaxies come into view. Then a thousand galaxies come into view.

Ten thousand galaxies come into my sight. Still my consciousness continues to expand.

A hundred thousand galaxies come into view.

A million galaxies come into view.

Then a single galaxy looks like a star.

Ten million galaxies come into my sight.

A hundred million galaxies come into view.

Countless galaxies form many clusters of galaxies.

A billion galaxies come into view.

Still my consciousness continues to grow.

Ten billion galaxies come into view.

A hundred billion galaxies come into my sight.

Still my consciousness continues to expand.

Then, there is nothing outside of me.

I come to the end of the universe.

"Seraph!" I call.

The Seraph appears on the other side of the universe about the same size as me.

As usual His body glows silvery, and He spreads His majestic six wings.

"Where are we now?" I ask.

"We are no longer in the dimension of the universe. We are in a different dimension."

"Why are we here now?" I asked the Seraph, while holding the whole universe with both hands.

"Because that is what you want. You want to heal and be in harmony with the universe," says the Seraph.

"I understand. I do feel healed. Thank you very much"

When I say that and opened my eyes, I am in my room. The clock shows 6:50 AM.

My morning healing program is over. I go to work as usual.

I say again "Thank you Seraph. Thank you, Ruth."

* * *

Taraku is a Level VI Seraphim Blueprint Teacher, a Ritual Master, 3rd step, an Advanced Healer, a Master of Crystology, and a Medical Doctor.

Emine's Story

I spent the first thirty-five years of my life occasionally getting angry, sometimes searching for happiness, and often allowing emotional choices to scatter my energies. I also experienced pleasure by disposing of difficulties with warrior courage and the ability to solve problems. My body was not getting used to this routine, however, and I got sick pushing the limits of my strength.

Even now, I can't forget those two years when breathing—a luxury for me—became a priority. I didn't believe in miracles—even so, I came across energies whose effectiveness I couldn't confirm. After a few breathing sessions, I could finally draw deep breaths. At the same time, odd things began to happen: interesting dreams competing with film scenarios and full of special signs. There was a voice telling me what I should and should not do; it was unsettling me and driving me to see the right way as a mother would do.

An unseen power was creating new scenarios. Despite denials from my analytical brain, I found myself directed by that voice. Through all these changes, I was taking lessons from a spiritual teacher and became a novice healer.

Throughout my life, I have been strong and self-confident; but now, as the disciple of a healer, I was learning to swim in a huge ocean. Dependent on my teacher, it took a long time to heal. After a while, the voice prompted me to take a different road. The voice was advising me to search for Seraphim energy. I had no idea what that meant. When I asked my teacher, she said I should look for energy different from hers. In my meditations, I heard voices even beyond those I'd been hearing in my dreams. I had a choice: I could wait for my teacher's advice, or I could listen to the voice and go on without fear. When I asked my heart, even the word "Seraphim" gave me a warm feeling and the belief that I was on the right path.

After a brief search on the Internet and a short telephone call, I heard that a Seraphim teacher, who rarely came to Turkey, was coming to my city to teach. That was a sign! Only a week later, a course was offered. In great excitement, I reached the course location without listening to cautions from my teacher. I was sorry when I realized that other applicants couldn't come, and I was the only one attending. Later, my teacher's words gave me joy when she said, "You eliminated all the others. Maybe you should get this teaching alone."

During the first initiation, a voice welcomed me, and that made me realize I was in the right place, and that this course was a turning point for me. For the first time, I saw a vision of one of my own past lives, and this made me happy because I had much more of everything in some of those lifetimes than I had in my current life.

After the course, I experienced great miracles. I could communicate with stones and read their memories; and when I touched people, I knew what kind of stone or crystal they needed. Mostly, the seraphim helped me to banish my fears. Then, my path and my teacher's separated, and I sailed in a new direction. What comforted my soul was talking about these newly discovered energies and this journey. Realizing my spiritual journey and discovering why I came here filled my inner emptiness.

My spiritual duty was to be a traveler. While travelling, I was meeting people, giving Seraphim teachings, and experiencing miracles afterwards. When I had learned this system, I wondered how I could see the teacher, dear Ruth Rendely. But since I had a fear of flying, I was hesitant to travel so far to her home. However, the Seraph showed me more miracles. During the 12-hour flight from Istanbul, I experienced the energies of the land of the Seraphim. In this mystic land, my dream showed me the reason for my phobia and the depth of dear Ruth's heart, and these gave me a unique friendship with Ruth.

In America Emine was reborn. After returning to Turkey, I travelled more, accompanied by my spiritual guide. In every city, I was meeting with people searching for themselves, and the most interesting thing of all was to find myself as a teacher of people gathered together by an unseen power. I was releasing them to the Seraph with the peace of total trust, and so I never advertised my teaching. When the students, in growing numbers, shared their experiences and miracles, I was reminded of my own journey of finding myself and getting a taste of my future life.

The Seraph was leading us to a kind of unity consciousness that God expects from all of us. The people taking the courses were sharing that same feeling as well. I realized that traveling across borders and cities for great distances was not tiring me, even as I was experiencing the greatest excitement that I cannot describe.

Sometimes while travelling on a bus, I realized that an unknown hand was organizing the passengers sitting nearby. I will never forget about one of those rides. The bus attendant approached me and told me that he saw a white light while serving me and that the stress that he'd had the past two years was lifted. Finally, he confessed a desire to stay in touch with me, and that is the reason why he was constantly asking to have coffee with me during that journey. Because of this confession, I was pleased to spend a half an hour healing him without feeling fatigue.

These kinds of meetings became part of my life, and I kept a notebook about them. Who knows? One day, I hope, this notebook will be an important legacy for following generations. Accompanied by my little suitcase on unknown routes, I was travelling continuously and willingly. Once my students from Çanakkale gave me a larger and sturdier suitcase when one of my courses coincided with my birthday. Although a suitcase is not on the top of a list of what a woman desires, not only did it make me happy, but it also was a sign of more future travels.

One of the most effective and unusual invitations I received was to a small village full of bucolic energy enhanced by the sounds of roosters crowing and lambs bleating. During my time teaching there, I was healed physically with the help of local food. Every time I went back there my brother searched for that same local food.

One night, when I realized that I could not respond to the need for Seraphim training in such a large part of the country, I prayed. In answer to them, two groups I taught asked me how they could become teachers. I smiled when I remembered the wisdom of the elders that "The way to be a master is the way to grow masters." The universe was eager to share its secrets with me, opening the doors for us while we were sharing what we had with others. No human brain can bear such a heavy load alone.

Finally, when I had trained my first teachers, I felt like a proud parent whose children had achieved good careers. We created a new Seraphim family and we were ready to meet with new people.

As I was struggling to write down this story, the same inner voice I'd heard before encouraged me and gave me a pen. Despite my fear that I could not write in the time left, I went ahead. While I was sitting in a small cafe, the words flowed onto a piece of paper that I had asked the waiter for. My story, in outline form, was waiting to be written, and I gathered a group together to provide me with the technical preparation to do so. During that training, I was not surprised when one of my talented students, Zeynep, asked me to stop because she felt that she had to begin with the Seraphim education first. She realized something strange and indicated her willingness to communicate with a bright light nearby in the room. Due to the curiosity of other students wondering what kind of experience this was, I instructed them into knowledge about the Seraphim.

The interesting thing was that I had the Seraphim book in my bag together with other books, but could not remember that I'd put it there. I understood that spiritual energy was just that sort of thing. It is not related to time, dimension, or space. It finds whoever needs it at the right moment. Who knows how, when, and where I will experience more and more to write in my notebook?

That night, I took my pen again and finished my whole

story. I realized that I was still carrying around my other commercial name due to my worldly, material fears, and so I left this belief behind. Without resisting, I keep following the ways presented by the universe.

Nowadays I am only dedicated to spiritual teaching. With every breath, I inhale all of life deeply. Who can say a disciple healer like me will become a successful traveling teacher, gathering many students to experience a life of miracles? Miracles continue to go on and on. I am not afraid of making mistakes anymore because I have a guide who has allowed me to experience a second life.

* * *

Emine Karakurt was born in 1977 in Afyon city in Turkey. She graduated from the faculty of Business Administration and Management, specializing in human resources .Her interests have been photography and self-realization. She is a Seraphim Blueprint Teacher who practices many different healing modalities

My Journey to
the Seraphim

I had been experiencing things over the past few months—things not of this dimension. I was seeing things that I could not explain, such as light orbs floating across the room and then disappearing into thin air. They came in different sizes, usually about the size of a pea to a marble, but, every now and then, a larger one, about the size of golf ball, would appear. Some were white; some different shades of pink and light blue; sometimes a combination of the colors; sometimes they would change colors as they floated by; and I would just sit there like, really? Did I just see that?

Sometimes Sandy and I were on the couch watching TV, and I would see one floating by, so I would look at her quickly, trying to catch her reaction, as the "marble" drifted right in front of her. Surely, she saw it—nope, nothing. Every now and then, I would see them, and they would be so bright, the brightest tiny light you could imagine, the size of a ball point pen tip; and it would be zipping across the room very fast, only to disappear into the wall—gone. I knew there was nothing wrong with my eyes, and there certainly wasn't anything wrong with my ears; yet I could hear people, who were not there, shouting at me too. I think that this drove me bonkers more than anything, as I couldn't understand what they were trying to tell me. It was like thirty people all shouting orders at once with their hands over their mouths—just that muffling, mumbling, shouting in a tunnel. What the heck was this all about? Isn't it enough that I am seeing things I can't talk about to anyone, but now I have voices shouting at me; I did think I was going nuts there for a while.

Things began to spiral out of control quickly; the medication I was on, 10 different pills per day, was making me very sick. I couldn't make it to work without pulling over and vomiting on the side of the road. I would be using my chipping hammer at work, and it would just fly right out of my hand due to the lack of sensation in my hands. I was using a grinder one day, and I had thought I had a good hold of it; nope, it shot out of my hands and into my stomach, the grinding wheel tearing through my coveralls and wading up in my shirt. Wow, close one! It wasn't long after when I was given an ultimatum from my employer: either show up to work or resign; or we will have to let you go. I had been fighting this for a year and a half now; my leave time was gone with every pay check; I had burned up all my short- as well as my long-term disability. I understood their view, as they had been very gracious throughout this whole ordeal, going above and beyond. Five days later, I turned in my letter of resignation. I finally felt like I had hit the bottom and had nowhere else to turn.

That couldn't have been further from the truth: I had more to go through before hitting the bottom. I remember lying in bed, curled up in a ball and crying; the pain was so intense. Sandy did everything she could to console me, but the slightest touch from her sent a shock of pain through me that was unbearable. I wanted her to touch me, but instead shouted out, "Just leave me alone; there is nothing you can do." Sandy would get up and go to work, and I would just lie or sit there all day in pain, seeing light orbs, shadow people appear and walk by, hearing voices, constantly seeing numbers everywhere, 9:11, 10:10, 11:11, 12:12, 2:22, 3:33, 6:15 (that's my birth date 6/15) and a few other combinations. I would see these signs everywhere.

After a while, planning my death seemed like the only thing I had going for me. There were times I would be lying there, looking at my pistol, and begging for the strength to go outside, walk off into the woods, and just end it all. Sandy and I both would be freed from this nightmare; she could hopefully move on, and I would be done with all the pain. We were both done; the look on our faces said it all when she would come home from work and ask, "What did you do today?" Or "How was your day?" I would reply in my grumpy negative way, "I sat here in pain all day, didn't do anything," or, "Same old shit as usual, how was yours?"

I knew I had to do something, or it was going to get real ugly real soon. Suicide was the easy way out, and it's about all I thought of. Taking my pills one day, it really hit me, and I pulled all the bottles out and lined them up on the counter. Wow, here I was contemplating taking my own life, and the doctors were just assisting me. At that moment, I grabbed all the bottles and threw them in the garbage. I was done taking all this crap; none of them were working anyway. The withdrawal was interesting to say the least: my emotions were up and down like a roller coaster, one minute fine, the next I was like: better get away from me. I started to consider holistic healing, and proper nutrition to try to fix my body.

I'd been told I had an arthritic illness. So, perhaps, the weather plays a part in it as well. They say warm and dry weather helps, and Alaska is anything BUT warm and dry! Desperate to try anything, I bought a ticket back to Las Vegas to stay with family for a while to see if the weather would help. But first, we'd had a trip planned, months in advance, to Hawaii. Hawaii although not dry, it is warm, so perhaps this would be a great little test to see about the weather theory.

The day we left for Hawaii, I was feeling pretty good; the pain level was very low, and the thought of getting out of Alaska in the middle of winter was very inviting. We arrived in Hawaii and checked into our hotel. Things were going great, the trip was wonderful until day four, and then things got so bad, I never recovered. Day four brought in heavy rains and the humidity shot up. Waking up on the fifth day, I could feel that pain coming on again: oh boy, here we go! Sure enough, it had started, and then it escalated. It was getting to the point where walking was just about impossible, and my attitude went south in a hurry, which did not make our time together any better. Sandy and I were in our hotel room, lying on separate beds and playing games on our phones, when she received a text from a friend who was also in Hawaii. She said that there was a psychic lady on the street who was good. She was about to pack up and leave, but said she would wait for us. Right off the bat, our answer was, "No." We were both just not in the mood, and then in a split-second, I heard "YES, GO," and I shouted to Sandy to tell the lady to wait, that we were on our way!

We got dressed and shuffled our way down the main drag. We had a way to go, and I was thinking, "Man, this is killing me, ouch," but I was pulled by an unknown force to keep going. We arrived at the spot to see an elderly woman sitting on a mat on the sidewalk with Tarot cards. At first. I thought, "Huh, this lady looks shady," but we paid her. Sandy went to chat with a friend while I sat down. I will never forget the eye contact we made, it was like a magnet to steel, and this lady just looked into my soul and beyond. I will admit, it was creepy, but I couldn't resist staring at her eyes.

She asked me to shuffle the cards and make six stacks in order, and it did not matter how many cards per stack. I did, and she picked up the first card, and, without looking at it, she shook it in my face and said in very firm voice, "Stop worrying about money! Enough already, your fear." My first thought was, "My gosh, is this my mother yelling at me?" I felt scolded. Then I realized she was right, I've been non-stop bitching about spending too much money. And then she drew the next card, and then the next one, and did it again until she had read every top card from the six stacks. I sat there in complete disbelief; there was no way this lady could have known this much about me. Impossible! But she did, she read me like a kindergarten book! She finished the reading, and I was floored. I quickly asked her to do a palm reading and paid her. She did, and again the things she told me were amazing! I knew this lady could help me, and so I asked her to please answer a couple questions; I would gladly pay her. She could see the desperate look on my face and looked at me with that look again, like she already knew what I was going to say. She said, "Keep your money, what is it you wish to know?" I told her about the orbs I see, the voices I hear, the numbers all the time, the shadow people I see, and the horrible dreams I have, only to see them played out on the

TV news or in the newspaper. She smiled at me and said, "I want you to go look up the word 'visionary,' and that is all I can tell you, other than that you will be fine." And with that, it was Sandy's turn. I sat with our friend in amazement going over what I had just heard, and was still stunned. Sandy came over and said, "Wow, she is good!"

Sandy had classes for the next couple of days, and I found myself in the hotel lobby glued to my laptop, googling everything I could think of. One hit led to another, and another, and soon I found myself knee deep in sticky notes with all kinds of numbers and notes. It felt like an hour had passed, when, in truth, it had been many hours, and it was time to go meet Sandy. We went to dinner and chatted about some of the things I had learned, and soon headed back to the hotel.

Two weeks after getting back from Hawaii, I was heading to Las Vegas in hopes the dry hot weather would be the cure. I could tell Sandy was ready for me to go too; we were at each other all the time. My negativity was draining her and was sending me into that black hole of darkness. I didn't really care what happened, so long as something happened.

Sandy took me to the airport and dropped me off; I remember that it was a weird feeling to say "goodbye." The look on her face was happy and full of hope that I would get healthy again; yet it was also sad with the fear that there might be no change. Even the hug and kiss were awkward; it felt like I was losing a part of her and of and me; it was hard to explain.

Landing in Las Vegas, I was greeted by my Mom and somewhat warm weather; it was the middle of February, sunny, and in the sixties. Driving to my Mother's house, I had this gut feeling that hell wasn't over, and this visit was going to be tougher than I'd thought. I didn't know it at the time, but I started to be consumed with fear. I started the dreaded "what-ifs": What if I don't get better? What if Sandy and I don't make it? What if.... These questions of doubt played in my head repeatedly like a broken record, and I let them control the way I felt daily; I was lonely, sad, angry, doubtful, and hopeless; in short, I felt worthless.

I awoke from this crazy dream one morning and was in awe; I lay there thinking "Whoa, what was that all about?" It was so surreal, very vivid in color and detail, but as if someone had taken a big paint brush and gently stroked it across the canvas I'd been painting, making it look a bit soft or hazy.

I was standing at the end of a runway, staring out at the ocean. I was floating off the ground about a foot with my arms straight out to my sides. Jetliners were taking off right next to me; I could feel the jet wash rumbling in my chest as they lifted off and flew out of sight over the ocean. I could smell the fuel from the exhaust fumes. Then, without warning, one of them crashed, slamming down into the water and breaking in half behind the wings right in front of me. Everyone survived, and I drifted away.

About a month later while sipping my coffee, I checked my email, and right there, on the front of the Yahoo news page, was a story of a plane that just had crashed in Bali. It had missed the end of the runway, crashing into the ocean and breaking in half right behind the wings, coming to rest in the exact same position as I saw it in my dream. Everyone survived. WOW! Are you kidding me! Another prophecy; this is crazy. I just sat there stunned, reliving that dream and reading the article. I wondered if I'd had a hand in saving all souls on board; else, why would I have been standing there, floating off the ground with my arms spread out like a cross? Am I a reincarnated saint of some sort? It's an interesting thought—one I may never know the answer to.

My psychic abilities were becoming fine-tuned, and it seemed that I had a touch of that ability in all the senses, which some would call, "super psychic." While I thought that this was all very cool and fun, I still didn't understand any of it. One night Mom and I were watching TV, sitting about eight feet apart in different chairs, and, out of the blue, the smell of cigarettes was very strong, as if someone were smoking right next to me. I asked, "Do you smell that?" Mom said, "Smell what?" I said, "Cigarette smoke.

She sniffed, "No, I don't.

I said, "Someone is smoking a cigarette right next to me, right here!"

She said it must be coming from outside. I went out, but there were no neighbors; nobody was around, and I could not smell it. I walked back inside, and right there again, the smell of cigarettes. Huh, strange. Mom said grandpa smoked, maybe he was visiting me. "Perhaps," I thought.

Having time on my hands wasn't helping and the "what ifs" came back to haunt me. I jumped online to google things to do in Las Vegas. Sandy and I had done some paranormal investing down in Arizona, and we'd loved it, so I searched for people in Vegas in hopes of hooking up with a few who were busy in some investigations of paranormal phenomena. I came across "Meet-Up" online and got lots of hits for different paranormal groups. So, I signed up and began perusing the many groups, sending a few messages to some, asking to join them on an outing or two.

I found a hiking group and joined, as they were having a hike in Red Rock coming up soon, and it sounded like it would be a great day. While looking around, I came across this place called "the Ganesha Center." I was checking out their calendar and noticed they had a lot of classes on the kinds of things I was going through, so I signed up with this group too.

The night before the hike, my ankle swelled up, and it was killing me. I thought, "Great, first chance to get out and do something and I am going to have to cancel." I took some Advil and went to sleep. I awoke to a new day, and, to my surprise, my ankle was much better, and I could go. The hike was great, and Red Rock is a spectacular place to visit. We all agreed to go have lunch afterwards and meet at a restaurant called the 'Yard house' at Red Rocks Casino.

There was about fifteen of us, and I sat at the very end of table, where I was joined by a lady, and she started some general chit chat. She was surprised that I was from Alaska and asked how I got to Vegas. I thought, "Make the story short, and she might not get too freaked out by all the psychic stuff and think I'm some kind of weirdo. After telling her a short version of my story, she said, "Wow, ME TOO!" Then she added, "You should go check this place out called the Ganesha Center"; baffled, I stated that I'd already found the place, but hadn't been there yet. She said, "Yes, you have to go; you will learn a lot about what's going on with you."

A couple days later, I went to the Ganesha Center and took a class called "Meditation with Angels"; it was fantastic! After class, I ran into the lady I'd met at lunch; we sat down for a minute to talk about the class I'd just taken, and she said, "If you liked that, you will love the Seraphim Blueprint course. Actually, I think the Seraphim Blueprint course is exactly what you need; it will help you greatly!" Not knowing anything about it, I saw that there was a free introductory class to be held soon, so I signed up.

The day finally came when I got to see what this Seraphim Blueprint hype was all about. I went to the Ganesha Center, checked in, and was directed to a room where the class was to be held. Walking in, I was greeted by a lady with a huge smile and a happy glow about her. She introduced herself to me as Brenda, and kindly asked me to have a seat. The class got underway with about five or six people eagerly staring at Brenda and all ears tuned in. She began to speak, and everything around me just seemed to stop; her smile and that happy upbeat voice were gentle and smooth, and she spoke with such confidence that you couldn't help but want to listen.

Brenda went into the history on how the Seraphim Blueprint energy came to be, explaining that it was an angelic healing energy that could be used by virtually everyone for the healing of themselves as well as others. The first level, Seraphim Healing, has two major energies, "Life Force Energy" and "Divine Harmonizer." Each has several "Attune-ments," and each Attunement, or energy, has a specific use. It was all Greek to me; I mean, Angels? Energy healing? I had no clue what I was hearing or the basis of any of it. Brenda then asked if we would like a sample of the energies. We all agreed, of course, and we closed our eyes, taking in a couple of deep cleansing breaths and sat there waiting; we didn't have to wait long; in a matter of seconds, BAM, it hit me! And I had no clue what to think. My mind was racing, trying to figure this all out. I was electrified, buzzing; waves of this kept coming in and out like waves lapping the shoreline. What in the heck was this? It lasted only a few minutes and was gone. I opened my eyes and was like, wow. Brenda was looking around at everyone with that smile of hers, and, by the look of the others, they got it too. We had a small discussion about what we felt and got some more information about the Seraphim Blueprint, and that ended the evening. Leaving, I knew this was for me; I just didn't know to what extent, yet.

At that time, levels one through five cost $160.00 each, and that I didn't have. I made a comment online about the class and how much I enjoyed it, but that I could not afford it now. Brenda replied with, "Just RSVP for the class; it will help you manifest the money!" So, I did, even though I knew nothing about "manifesting," or where the heck the funds for this were coming from.

I started taking other small classes that were free or very low cost and started to understand more of what was going on. I took several meditation classes, which turned out to be a huge help. Not only were those voices quieting down, but when they came in, they were clear, and I could hear and understand what they were telling me. These classes really opened my psychic abilities, and this kept me coming back for more. I spent hours reading every day, gathering more information, and searching for more answers. I meditated for an hour every day as well, but I still couldn't get all of it. No matter how much reading and meditating I did, I still wasn't happy with what I found. "There has to be more, right?" That's what I kept thinking.

I had locked myself within and was looking for the key to get out, not realizing the key is always right there, within. I was in a new state, had a fiancé back in Alaska, a relationship that had been stressed to the breaking point, and there was no clear light at the end of the tunnel. I always seem to have this tiny flicker of flame left inside though and continue, day in and day out, to feed it, soothing it to stay lit: faith?

Sandy called me up one day and said there was a guy who wanted to buy my snow machine. "SOLD," I said in a relieved and excited voice! Just three days before Seraphim Blueprint Level 1, the money somehow appeared from the sky, like a gift, at the right time. Excited about getting to attend, I drove down to the Ganesha Center and paid for the class. Now, only a couple more days of anticipation!

I awoke on the morning of April 7, 2013 with much excitement. I did my meditation, showered, ate breakfast, grabbed my stuff, and headed out the door. Upon arrival, I was escorted to the room where the class was to be held. As I walked in, I was surprised to see so many people; the room was packed. I was the only male; this did not shock me, as I was used to being the only male in several classes I had been to. That's too bad; I think that more men need to open to what they have inside, rather than relying on what's on the outside all the time. I made a comment about being the only guy and that this did not surprise me, as I sat at the end of the room, and one of the ladies belted out, "Yea, we know why you're here," and a couple of the ladies chuckled. Ahhhhh yes, people read the cover of a book and take it for gospel all too often, but that's ok.

The class started with members introducing and telling a bit about themselves. It was interesting to hear why everyone else was there; while everyone's story was different, they were also similar. My turn came, and I started in on why I thought I was there (really had no clue to be honest, other than someone said it would be good for me), and everyone's attention tuned in, as I spoke of my psychic abilities and what I was going through. Not tooting my own horn, but the look on their faces were priceless, especially from the lady who'd belted out that she knew why I was there, and with that, I gave the floor back to Brenda. Just as she started to speak, there was a gentle knock at the door, it opened, and in walked another gentleman. "Whew, cool, I'm not the only guy in this class after all," I thought.

After a brief introduction of herself, Brenda asked us to close our eyes, take a deep breath, and take a few minutes to become grounded. As I did, I could feel myself calming down and coming back to the here and now. I was still unsure of all this angel stuff and had a bit of doubt, but was eagerly ready to find out. Brenda began the class.

She read from the Level 1 handout, "Life Force Energy," and you could feel the energy change in the room; it was getting warmer, and I sensed that we were not alone; some being had joined us. As Brenda finished the first part of her read, she said it was time to take the first Attunement or Initiation. I got comfortable, closed my eyes, took in a deep breath, released it, and drifted off to wherever it was I was to go.

Within seconds I could feel waves of energy coming and going; my hands were pulsating; my brow chakra was opening, and visions started coming in forms of colors swirling around like fire dancing. Very soon those colors formed a shape, a face, and as it drifted closer to me, it began to become crystal clear it was an Angel!

He had long grey hair flowing down, a bushy beard with

a moustache, and piercing blue eyes. He came so close, it was like he was sitting two feet in front of me, just looking at me with a gentle smile. I remember feeling at complete peace! And that was a wonderful feeling to have. He stayed there for about a minute, long enough to give me messages, and thank me for finally showing up; an understanding that I was doing the correct thing by acknowledging him came over me.

He then slowly drifted off, up and to the left, and disappeared. Moments later, I could feel the energy change, and seconds later Brenda stated that the initiation was over, to please bring our awareness back into the room, and to open our eyes when we were ready. I thought to myself, "Yeah right, come back, and are you nuts? I was in heaven! Let me stay!" But I did come back. We spent some time sharing our experiences with each other and enjoying the journey.

There are 13 Attunements within the two energies of level one; "Life Force Energy" and "Divine Harmonizer." First initiation down, twelve more to go, and I was blissed out of my mind already. I was still in a bit of shock, sitting there, going over in my mind what just happened, how clear it had been, so real. I said to myself, "This just can't be, that couldn't have happened? Or did it?"

We got comfortable and readied ourselves for the second Attunement. Breathing in a deep cleansing breath, I closed my eyes and waited for the next unknown. Like the first one, it started off with visions of colors swirling about, sensations of waves flowing throughout the body; I was in pure relaxation and enjoyment when, BOOM! With a thunderous entrance, right before me at my feet, he arrived. It was such a loud boom, that I could feel the ground shake! In a split tenth of a second, I almost shot up and opened my eyes, it was THAT startling! There he was, standing before me, towering above me. I felt like an ant on the sidewalk gazing upon this giant being; I just kept looking up, and up, seeing every crystal-clear speck of this angel before me. Easily, he was thirty feet tall, eight to ten feet wide at the shoulders, muscular, with a light bronze glow. Looking down upon me, he knew I saw him, and knew that I would never doubt his existence again. He cracked the slightest grin in confirmation, spread his wings, shot up and was gone in a split second. When I opened my eyes, Brenda's eyes were right there to greet mine; it was like she knew what this was meant for me; she smiled, knowing that I just had another grand experience. Boy, did I ever; such an experience, that tears of joy are flowing as I write this; I will never forget this moment, the moment I knew what I was meant to do, here, on this planet, Earth; love!

I know it may sound strange to some, or most, but I can honestly say I had never felt such true love as I did at that moment. I was completely floored and blown away by the raw power of an emotion I have taken for granted for so long: love. Once one feels the pure essence of this magnificent emotion, one is blessed.

When it was my turn to share, the first thing I said was, "How do I become a teacher of the Seraphim Blueprint?" And Brenda explained: after you take all six levels, you fill out an application and mail it to Ruth (the most recent founder of the Seraphim Blueprint), and she will connect with the Seraph and get his guidance. If you are approved by the Seraph, you have two years to complete the teacher's training, or you need to reapply. Well, I knew what I was doing, my plan was set, and the next chapter in my life had just opened: teaching the Seraphim Blueprint.

I explained what I had seen and felt to the class, and they sat there in amazement, asking why they hadn't seen such things, and how did I do it? I had that deer-in-the-headlights look, staring into a deep tunnel; "I don't know," I said. "It just happens; it just appears; I'm not sure how or why I do what I do, or even if I know?" I felt like I wanted to just leave the class at that point and go sit somewhere alone and stare at nothing while I figured this all out. My life had just been touched in a way that, to this minute, I can't explain. That's how I know how beautiful of a moment it was; it's unexplainable; because it was meant to be 'felt', not explained. Now it still touches me so very deeply and it fills my heart with such gratitude! I guess if I had one wish in life, it would be for everyone to be touched in this way; then and only then do I think we all could live together, as one.

The rest of the day continued to be amazing: Attunement after Attunement, I could feel my inner body shifting, so many thoughts going through my mind, so much to figure out, so much to understand; expansion at its finest was happening.

I took all the levels and retakes. Heading to Naples, Florida for teacher training was a big leap, another new chapter opening. This journey has been the biggest in my life; it has reinforced 'trust' into my soul, that there are good things in this life; you just need to listen to your angels. . . .

* * *

Curt Buettner was born in Limestone, Maine and at the age

of six months, his father 's Air Force assignment transferred the family to Anchorage, Alaska, where he grew up and lived for 44 years. From the age of five, which is the earliest he can remember, he has always believed in angels. He currently lives in northwestern Georgia, and still finds himself in the middle of Spiritual Growth; with much gratitude to the Seraphim Angel, "S".

Noah's Diary Entry

My seventh birthday will be in a couple days. I've been seven years in this body! I've done this Phase so many times. It used to be difficult to survive on this planet. The human body is weak and vulnerable, but every individual unit contributes to a gene pool which is incredibly potent and driven by an urge to procreate. The body thrives with every new generation. The human brain is surprisingly capable. It helps humans to improve their living conditions, which, in turn, improves the longevity of the body. Although humans still struggle to exceed Phase Thirteen, which equals 91 years on Earth, it has become much easier now to stay longer in the same body.

The first Phase is difficult, because, even if you carefully chose the DNA components of your physical body, once you enter it and take your first breath, you are exposed to many complex forces of various sources. It takes time and effort to adjust. While you try to adapt to the gravity and density of this planet, you are completely dependent on adults to survive. That's one of the reasons why you need to choose your parents wisely. But that's not enough. The coordinates you will be born into can be even more important. So do your research well.

Fortunately, after birth, the human body is on autopilot for a while, which is convenient. It gives you time to figure out how to run it. Once you settle in, you start with the basics—like moving your limbs, feeding yourself and communicating. Telepathy is dormant in humans; you need to learn vocal speech. That's not easy! During my first couple of lifetimes, it took me nearly halfway through the first Phase until I could get a grip on this. Be patient.

But there is a catch. Every time you learn something new in the physical realm, you lose a part of your spiritual memory. The longer you stay in this reality, the weaker your connection to your true Self becomes. At some point, during the first two Phases, you completely forget who you really are. You feel like you are detached from everything. Creation has disowned you and sentenced you to exist on your own. You experience plain singularity. It is an exceptional experience, worthy of undergoing, but it is hard to exist that way. You feel lost, and your life-source gets weaker.

When you start to communicate with other humans, stick to their lingo and their topics. Ask questions, rather than answering theirs. Don't try to share your wisdom. Trust me. That way you avoid lots of trouble and save time. The first couple of times, when I finally could talk, I got really excited, because I wanted to bond with the humans around me. I opened up, and told them what I was going through. All I got in return was fear, strict rules, boundaries, disbelief, and resistance.

Fear rules this planet, by the way. You can easily get addicted to it. To be able to thrive despite fear, humans created various control and defense mechanisms, and they cling to them collectively. Therefore, it is quite a challenge to form an identity that is true to your purpose on this planet. Your gifts, qualities and spiritual heredity are squashed into the limiting defense templates of the human mind. This is unbelievably painful. This pain radiates into all layers of your being: physical, emotional, mental and even into the subtlest levels. It eats up all your joy, trust, and curiosity. Yes, you lose your essential ties to Source, but you continue to exist in this reality. At least, your body does. That is one of the miraculous attributes of the human body and the human reality. It functions even off the grid. That is also one of the reasons why this reality is so chaotic.

As mentioned before, choose your parents wisely. Take your time. It is worthwhile to wait for the right ones. Yes, their DNA is important, because it shapes the body you run, but check their life purposes and future potential as well. It is tricky. If you are unsure, you can also look for a Phase Two or Three body. When you find one, try to make an agreement with the Occupier. Sharing a body can be very convenient. That way you get to skip the first two risky Phases, and since there is already someone running the body, you can watch and learn. I did that a couple times, but I rather like to form the personality of the individual body and to be able to do that, you must be alone during the first Phase. Last time I took on an Inserter at Phase Two. Maybe I will do that again. It is much more fun to have a partner. Collective qualities and experiences enhance the life potential of the human you are directing.

This time I chose two humans who were in Phase Six as my parents. That is the Phase where most humans start to remember. It is generally a vague memory, but enough to trigger a longing for something beyond themselves. They question their singularity and try to let go of fear. They become seekers. They may even find ways to kindle their dormant abilities and skills. My mother is trying to reach out to her outer layers. That is one of the reasons I picked her. I help her to open up. In return, she helps me to keep my link to spiritual consciousness. Well, that is the plan, and so far it is going well. For example, when I told her that I don't want to eat animals she did not force me to. Eating animals harms the human body's advanced senses, and after a while they shut down. When that happens, you are left with the default ones. You don't want this to happen, because without the advanced ones you lose the upper hand, and before you know it the body starts to act on its own. If you are not able to be the boss, you have no other choice than quitting and leaving the body. That means you are back to square one. So, I refused to eat meat and mother listened to me. Two years ago, when she put meat in front of me, I refused to eat. First, she resisted of course, and tried to trick me. But when she realized that I was determined, she gave up. After a while she also stopped eating animals. That has changed her entire energy flow, and since then her link to her subtle bodies has improved. She and I have some karmic residue to resolve in those layers, and having a healthy flow of energy throughout our energy bodies helps a lot. I really want to clear the blockages. That is the main reason I picked her as my mother. Hope I succeed.

Phases Two and Three are quite turbulent. The hormones kick in. Nothing can beat hormones. They take over and cut you out. The body becomes the boss. Phase Two and Three are a fast-track transformation into becoming an adult body. Like all types of DNA on earth, the human DNA is an incredibly potent director. It wants to procreate. It is an amazing experience, though, very intense. The mind is working overtime. You get adventurous and start to challenge your body's limits. Your physical senses are working perfectly; the body is at its best, so you go full throttle, discovering the reality you live in. But there is one major drawback: every new experience puts a new brick in the wall between human reality and your spiritual heritage. Your individual self grows and your link to unity gets weaker. You become self-centered, materialistic. That is the major characteristic of Phase Four. Somehow you imprison yourself in your own universe. Before you reach Phase Five you succumb to live in the illusionary reality of human consciousness.

So, when you finally reach Phase Six at age 35, not only will your physical body be pretty messed up, but your mind will also be completely assimilated to the rules and boundaries of the human status. That is what I have experienced so far in previous incarnations. The physical body shows signs of exhaustion, the emotional layer is full of blockages, and the mental layer is out of control. If you have been smart enough to partner with an Inserter during one of the previous Phases, you can take a break and relax for a while. Phase Six is no picnic, for sure.

Also, watch out for Karma traps. They lurk in every corner, disguised, insidious, and cunning. You need to curb your appetite for the material world and find your way back to your true Self, or you will get lost and end up in weird scenarios that do not have happy endings. You need to kindle the heart connection. Trust your gut; decide and act with your heart. These frequencies will lead you back to your true Self, but you need to get your conscious mind on board first.

Your conscious mind is like a bridge connecting the material to the transcendental. It's tricky, though. Do not get stuck there. I once did. It is in the realm of reason and control. It imprisons you and you lose precious time. Meditation is an effective way to avoid such a pitfall. It calms the mind, and with a quiet mind you can remove bricks from the walls you will have built around yourself by then. Be easy on yourself. You will have to remove many, many bricks. So be patient and continue to meditate. It is very effective. You will succeed. I promise.

Regarding Phases Seven and Eight, I don't have much experience yet. Last time, I had to leave my body at forty-six. That is the longest I managed to stay on Earth so far. My current parents were going through Phase Seven when I joined them. Now they have reached Phase Eight. So, I was able to observe. It looks like humans go through a second transformation during this Phase. Good to have a preview right now. The physical body gets weaker and the subtle layers start to recover. You get another chance to connect with your true Self. Having small children around also helps. I noticed that my energy bodies activate the heart chakras of my parents. It is an incredibly effective interaction. The heart chakra, once activated, opens the channels to the upper ones.

This time I am confident I will experience these Phases myself. Thanks to advances in technology, human life expectancy has finally been extended. Now we can experience Phases after Thirteen, which is very exciting. That is also the reason why there is such a huge demand for the human experience. Maybe I will be one of the first who gets that far?

"Noah, where are you, honey?"

That's my mom.

"In my room!"

There she is. Love it when she has these bright colors in her aura.

"You look busy?"

"Yeah, I am writing something down."

Yes, it has its perks to have done Phase One so many times. Started talking at fifteen months and could read and write at age five. It is nice to be treated like a Wunderkind.

"You want to share?"

I wish! But she is not ready. She is getting there, but she needs more time. I used to share my thoughts and feelings with her when I started talking. I hoped to jog her memory. We have the same cosmic origin, so I thought she would support me to unfold my true identity. Big mistake! She got very concerned, and, instead of remembering, she clung to the rules and boundaries of her illusionary reality. She got worried and suspicious and acted really weird. She even took me to some specialists to find out if there was something wrong with me. So, I gave up. I love her and don't want to make her worry. She already has to deal with a lot of stuff that distracts her from her true Self. It makes me sad when I see drab colors in her aura. She looks so beautiful when her aura is bright and shiny.

"Not yet, maybe later."

"Okay, we need to get ready for yoga class."

Love that she is doing yoga. It is a perfect way to clear the energy meridians of the human body. The body gets more and more flexible, and the more you realize how flexible you are the more you question all the rules and boundaries of human consciousness. Questioning boosts your awareness, and awareness is what sets you free. She takes me with her.

I support her with all my heart. All kids do that. At least the ones in the junior yoga class do. It's fun to help grown-ups to grow up.

"Can I take the glass stones to the yoga class? I want to show them to the other kids."

"What stones?"

"The ones you brought home yesterday. You left them on the table in the living room, and I took them. Here."

"Oh, those are called crystals, quartz crystals. You like them?"

"Yes! When I hold them, my hands start to tingle."

That is because of the frequency they emanate, I know. But you have to watch out how you express yourself at this age, rules and boundaries.

"Wow, how wonderful! You know what; I feel the tingling, too."

"Why do they make my hands tingle?"

Let's see how she is going to explain this to me.

"Well, yesterday I went to a class where I learned about energies that make us happy and healthy. They showed me how to put those energies into crystals, and I did that with the ones I brought home. Maybe the energies are the reason why you feel tingling and heat in your hands."

"Where do the healing energies come from?"

Silly question, but I am getting excited when mom discovers these kinds of things and I want her to take it seriously.

"Well, these are energies that come from very powerful, bright angels."

Humans have the primitive need to touch and feel things to include them in their reality. They love to embody energies. Very few of them can perceive the different vibrations and frequencies of creation. It is difficult to be able to pick them up in this dense, three-dimensional world, but the human brain steps in and, thanks to stored data, it creates tailor-made images and sensations for any energy it wants to perceive. Once it is recorded by the collective consciousness, it becomes a part of human reality. Any energy can have a form here. They give them names such as "angels," "dragons," "fairies." Be smart, play along, and stick to their lingo.

"So, does that mean I am touching an angel when I hold the crystal?" Do you get what I mean?

"Well, in a way you could say so," she smiles.

These energies come from a very high consciousness. They will help her to claim her true Self. Ironically, while she will strengthen her bond with her true Self, mine will get weaker and weaker.

"Can I take one with me?

"Sure. Take all of them. But..." she pauses, "...but, Noah, don't tell your friends about the energies, they may not understand, okay?"

Oh Mom! The kids do understand. The grown-ups are the problem here. But there is no point in telling her this. She wouldn't comprehend. These kinds of remarks damage your connection with higher consciousness and your true Self. Secrecy, obscurity, and disguise are feeding the material self.

"Don't worry; I just want to show them the crystals."

See. I am already complying.

Although I am excited that I am about to begin Phase Two, my feelings are bitter sweet. Like so many times before, this illusionary reality will take over and will overwrite and sensor my life's purpose.

"Let's go, Noah. We don't want to be late."

This time I will try to resist. I will continue to write all my thoughts and experiences down until it makes no sense to me anymore. Maybe it will help me remember; maybe it could help others remember? Or maybe I become a storyteller?

"I am ready, Mom."

* * *

Inspired by the beauty and power of the Seraphim Blueprint energies, Özden Öke became a Seraphim Blueprint teacher in 2013. She enjoys doing soul readings and translates spiritual books into Turkish. She loves gardening and spends most of her time in nature. She lives with her husband, three dogs and a cat in Istanbul, Turkey.

The Saint Within
My Heart

Human beings live their lives based on their perceptions. Life happens to them exactly the way they perceive it. Not one step different from that.

My story started with my willingness to move forward. There were times I took a break, and, instead of being actively involved, I preferred to watch my life as if it were a movie or a fantastic show.

Looking back, I can see that early in my life I had a strong ability to connect with higher dimensions. I remember that, mostly at night, I would experience angelic energies which I knew I was not imagining. They opened new doors for me, and I felt filled with love that poured into me like being in a lantern full of light. The angelic beings would encircle me with their energies and take me on journeys to fantastic realms until I woke in my bed the following morning.

I sought the saint within me throughout my life. Realizing that I was seeking him was like a miracle to me. I was unaware that the dream that I'd had at age nineteen would be a preview of my destiny.

My grandmother, who lived with us, was a respected,

wise woman. She carried lots of stories in her experienced heart. On a snowy winter day, the 13th of February, she told me that this day was very important and special. She said that if I would fast until sunset and not drink even a drop of water until I went to bed, I would be able to see a saint in my dream, who would take me to a spring; or a person would give me water who would become my husband.

As you may have guessed, at age nineteen, I was instantly intrigued and decided to follow her directions. I fasted that day until sunset and did not drink any water until I went to bed. I had a hard time falling asleep. Finally, around 4:45 in the morning, I fell asleep…

THE DREAM

I was in a pool. I felt the water, but could not see it. There was water, but it was transparent like air. My friends from university, Berrin and Berna, were with me. They both showed me the wedding rings that they had found in the pool. But I was busy observing the water. I was so amazed that it looked like air.

Then, like in a movie, the scene changed, and I found myself on a narrow staircase. It looked like the stairs of a minaret. Although I never had been in a minaret before, a voice inside me said: "You are in a minaret." The stairs were narrow, tiny, and like a spiral.

Narrow as the staircase was, it was packed with people who were rushing down. It was chaotic. Everybody was in a hurry. I, on the other hand, was calm and looking at the people who were pushing each other. Slowly, I also went down.

Suddenly, we were all outside. It looked like half the population of our planet was there. It was like the Sahara Desert. The minaret we'd left was very small. I wondered how we had fit in it and why we were there. We stood there back to back, side by side, as if we'd been placed in a scattered arrangement. Then my eyes grew wide open. I was in awe when I suddenly saw a beautiful turquoise-colored sea in the middle of the desert and right in front of us.

We stood there quietly, admiring the beauty of the sea and waiting for something to happen. All the people in the crowd were different. They were so many—men and women from different cultures with different skin colors.

And then, a huge, black angel with a covered face appeared at the shore of the sea. The angel told us that we would see the greatness of the sea soon. He said, "If your heart is filled with goodness and pure love, do not be afraid, the sea will only touch your feet." (My inner voice told me that the sea would recognize what kind of person we are when the water touches us). The Angel continued: "If the opposite is true, all that you have laid upon the earth will come back to you."

I was trembling. I felt fear, but I was also curious about what was going to happen. I heard a clattering noise deep inside me. My heart was beating like crazy. Maybe the noise I was hearing was the heartbeats of the others.

When the sea started to rise, the magnificent turquoise color turned black. It rose ten times its original size, and the waves, as if they had four dimensions, came upon us with an enormous force. My heart stood still; I didn't hear any noises anymore, and everybody was holding their breath. The angel stood there, while the waves came closer. I was watching all that was happening and thinking that, maybe, the waves would take me first. My fear vanished. I closed my eyes and surrendered to the moment. At that instant, maybe for a split second, I felt the sea touching my feet. The first thing I saw when I opened my eyes was the sea. It was turquoise and as serene and beautiful as it had been when I first saw it. When I looked around, I realized that half the people were gone. The sea had taken them. The angel was gone, and we were left there by ourselves.

Like the "cut" command of a film director this scene changed, and I found myself in a different location. This time, I was at my cousin's home. All the furniture was there, but why was this house so empty and without people? I was wondering. Then I saw myself in a mirror. The right side of my face had a scar. The scar went down in one stroke. I felt deep sorrow.

Suddenly, I found myself in another scene. I felt like an actress in a movie who doesn't know her lines and hasn't any clue what part she is playing. When I looked around, I realized that I was in a graveyard in the middle of the night. The same black angel showed up at my right. I asked him questions: "Where am I? Why am I here? Who are those people lying here…?" The angel responded, "A mother and her son... People mourned for them." I wanted to ask, "Why are you telling me this?" but I stayed quiet. Instead, with the spirit of a 19-year-old girl, I asked him a different question, "Hey, I am supposed to drink water. Why is there no water? My grandmother told me that my soulmate would give me water! She is never wrong. Where is my water?"

While I was babbling all these childish questions at the angel, I sensed that he was smiling, but I still couldn't see his face; I didn't feel the need.

"Look," said angel pointing up to the sky, "Your water is there."

I saw a bright star that dazzled my eyes! I heard myself shouting, "How beautiful!"

The star turned into the portrait of a man. He had black, curly hair and a hair band that went around his head. He was pouring me water. It felt like being washed by a bright, crystal-clear waterfall. I was bedazzled by his beauty.

THE NEXT MORNING

I woke up and hurried full of joy to my grandmother, "I saw him, I saw him. He gave me water." When she saw the glow in my eyes, she smiled. Then she calmed me down and said, "First, that's an amazing dream. There are lots of stories hidden in it. Your soul mate is like a star. But you must be faithful and patient to find him. You will recognize him when you see his light, and he will recognize you through your faith."

I felt disappointed when she told me to be patient. I interrupted her to ask if it would take long. My grandmother said, "You are going to experience all the visions you saw in your dream. Even if it takes a lifetime, do not ever give up on him. Do not lose faith; your faith is the key."

But I didn't take her words seriously. I had seen my soulmate, and the rest wasn't important.

FIVE YEARS LATER...

Berrin and Berna got married one after the other. (I never thought of my dream).

In 1999, on August 17th, a massive earthquake hit Istanbul. Many lives were lost that night. When we were carrying my grandmother down the stairs to leave the building, people were pushing us and almost ran over us. (I never thought of my dream).

In the year 2000, my cousin lost his wife. His wife had been my friend for ten years. He moved out of the house that they'd lived in together, thus making his house empty as it was in my dream. My cousin mourned for eight years. As a family, we found ourselves in the middle of deep grief. (I never thought of my dream).

Then, I suddenly remembered my dream. I remembered the order of the events. I was totally shocked. Oh, my god! I was living it!

While life was happening, I was searching for my star. I was looking for somebody who resembled him. But not all events I saw in my dream had manifested yet, so I knew I would have to wait.

In 2015, I was thinking of my dream once again. I had experienced all the events except one: The scene where I was in the graveyard looking at the graves of a mother and her son. I immediately got the shivers. I didn't want to live through that.

I was determined to find my star, but I wished to find him easily. In the fall of 2015 I had another dream.

2015 DREAM

This time I saw a brunet, curly-haired man in my dream. He told me that his name was "Ezekiel." We were at a train station; although there were trains, the station looked deserted. He was constantly moving and telling me to follow him, "Come with me."

I asked him, "Are you my star?

He was not answering. But he repeated, "I am Ezekiel."

I remembered that I looked at the ceiling for a while after I woke up. Then I saw my diary and opened a new page where I wrote, "Ezekiel."

I googled "Ezekiel" but couldn't find anything. Then I said to myself, "Well you were looking for your star, but now you have to find Ezekiel, too!" What kind of name is Ezekiel, anyway? It does not even sound like a 'human' name!"

Since I had been meditating for many years, I decided to ask for inner guidance during my meditations, but I got no response. I called upon the universe and repeated every day that I was looking for the saint within me. I wanted to find my star.

After a while, maybe because we are human, daily realities took over and I put all this aside.

I attended many training programs to improve my spiritual and personal growth. When I started with the "Seraphim Blueprint" workshops in the fall of 2016, I noticed that my meditations became more intense and I felt that I was evolving faster. Soon thereafter, in April of 2017, I became a teacher of the "Seraphim Blueprint." I still cannot believe how I was able to take all the steps so fast and become a teacher of my favorite healing system.

About two months ago, while I was meditating, an angel visited me for the first time. He was the same angel I had seen in my dream: the black angel who hid his face…. This time, he told me that his name was Ezekiel. And he added that he was "the Angel of Transformation." I never had experienced such a thing.

Ezekiel was an angel! I had seen an angel in my dream! With the excitement of the 19-year-old girl that I still carried within me, I contacted my spiritual meditation group to find out if this information was true. They confirmed it. Ezekiel is an Archangel!

The happiness and joy I felt I cannot describe. It's miraculous and magical! At the same time, I felt relieved because it was obvious that, soon, I was going to meet my star! But the last event in my dream, the graveyard of "mother and son," continued to weigh on me!

I was praying and begging my angels, "Please let me experience this last event in a very light way."

My cousin (who lost his wife in 2009) recently sent me a text message with a photo. He sent it to me while he was on vacation. Under the photo, he wrote, "This is the grave of "Mother and Son." People come here to mourn. Look, they are buried side by side."

As I am writing this I get goose bumps, as I got them when I read that text message.

I experienced all the events I saw in my dream. The universe responded to my prayers with the same unconditional love I feel in my heart, "Look, the last event happened as you wished; you passed through this experience in a very light way!"

And I am calling upon the universe once more:

"Dear Archangel Ezekiel, I am ready. I am looking for the saint within; I am looking for my star whose love I feel deep within my cells. I am ready to recognize his light and, as my late grandmother told me, he will be able to recognize me by my faith."

* * *

Sibel Esiyok from Istanbul, Turkey enjoys writing, reading and exploring what's good for her soul. She loves hugging trees and feeding animals. She discovered Seraphim Blueprint energies in the spring of 2016 and became a Seraphim Blueprint Teacher in 2017.

Wake Up!

"Wake up Nancy! Wake up! It is time to open your eyes." As the cherub-faced girl opened her dark-lashed, bright blue eyes, there was a palpable sigh of relief in the ICU.

I chose to come back and continue in this two-year old's body and to complete the mission the Light had assigned to me. While I was flat lining and being rushed to emergency surgery to save the life of the body I inhabit, I was cradled in the arms of an immense figure I only knew as Christ from a picture my Grandmother had on her wall. This figure and I were in the other world, the other dimension, where there is lightness and light. I know this world so well. I love to dance with the energy. I adore the feel of its caress on my etheric body and to know the interplay of the vastness of the energy that is the All. I did not want to come back. I chose to anyway. I had given my word to come and participate in a mission outlined in the All. I was just one part of a plan I did not need to know.

In the beginning, I was so excited to support this angelic plan, the plan of the Light, of the All. I was excited to emerge as a consciousness that would animate this body given me. I've done this before. I know this path. I know the journey ahead. It is such a brief bleep in the vastness of limitlessness, where there is no construct of time and space; where knowledge is – all is possible; where there is no meaning to construct, just construction; and where there is no duality, only oneness, connectedness and beauty of free interchange in the light, entangled in the interplay of love. This is the place you feel when you look deeply enough into anyone's eyes to feel their soul.

"Time to open those eyes beautiful one. It is your time to be here now in this dimension, this earthly journey." As the monitors in the pediatric ICU would sound, the nurses would come into the room and find little me in the cribs of the other children. They asked, "What are you doing lovely little girl?" I would say, "Healing the children. Just healing them." The nurses would laugh. They knew my mother well; she, too, was an emergency room nurse. They would tell her what I'd said and Mom would laugh and say, "I read her all those *Nurse Nancy* books; that is where she gets that from. Isn't it adorable she loves to pretend."

I was not pretending that Christmas season. No child was lost in the ICU during that week. They all chose to stay and fulfill their missions.

"You must heal the animals Nancy! You must speak for us!" This wise, enlightened soul embodied in a furry package named Hie Kie said to me one day. He was a wise friend: my horse. He and I spoke for hours out in the woods of Minnesota. He taught me to listen to the trees, plants, and other animals supporting Gaia and her mission to house and care for these human journeyers. I would lie on the ground and hear Gaia's heartbeat and her plea. I would hear the pleas of the plants, animals and stones. I would feel what they felt and feel so loved and loving all at the same time. I was connected to the plan.

"Mom! Guess what Hie Kie told me today?" I said with enthusiasm as I was running into the house. "What darling girl?" Mom said. "I am to heal the animals." I exclaimed with absolute certainty, determination, and humility for being sent on such a mission. I was ready to start that day. Then Mom said, "Wow! What a fantastic imagination you have!" I thought, "Oh. Is that what you call what I do when I talk with the plants and animals? I am a fabulous Imaginarium!"

The following years were concentrated on getting high grades and avoiding the abusive, alcoholic energies of the home. But I buckled down to become a veterinarian, so I could heal the animals. Mom told me the way to heal animals was to be a doctor. I was focused, determined, and directed. By my senior year, I had earned a full scholarship and was ready to set out. Hie Kie and I were off to college and the equestrian team. Hie Kie, among many other animals, had been my teacher of truth and the path I was honored to walk for the preciousness of Gaia and all she loved. Despite turbulent living conditions, I was poised to carry out the privilege to serve these souls I knew so well.

"Wake up Mom. Just Wake up." And then I pleaded with God, "Do not take my mom. I cannot do this if she is gone. Take me! Take away all my light and give it to her." Mom had inoperable lung cancer and six weeks to live. My Dad would not allow me to go to college.

Several days later, Hie Kie died unexpectedly. He was my confidant, my connection to light, my truth in this crazy, hard world filled with turmoil, darkness and hate. How could I do this anymore? How could I heal animals? Hie Kie was gone. I disconnected, unplugged and yet continued to pursue hard science, no longer the Imaginarium. My mom lived another sixteen years, mostly due to believing she would. I continued my promise to my dear horse to become a veterinarian and minister to animals. No longer willing to connect to the Light and listen, I knew it was my fault Hie Kie died. I asked for all my light to pour into my mom, and it did. Hie Kie had completed his mission; he saved my mom, which saved me from going down a path of darkness. It took me ten years to find my way back. To know, really know, that Hie Kie had only fulfilled his piece of a puzzle bigger than all of us. He had returned to the Light, to the All that is. Animals are embodied angels, here to support us on the mission we signed up for on this planet called Earth.

"Wake up Nancy!! Wake up Now!" All the animals began to scream at me. I had been a veterinarian for a few years then. I was disillusioned and often-in disbelief over the cruelty with which humans treat animals. I felt the failure to heal them. I had become so disillusioned, I was deathly ill and ready to leave my body. But these energies screamed at me. They sent me light, sent me back to the All. And this reawakened the Imaginarium. "Open Nancy OPEN!" I felt, I saw, I heard, and even tasted and smelt the messages they wanted to share. I reconnected to the angels, the energies, and the relationship to the All. I plugged back into the grid, the Oneness of the limitless vastness of the All. I had in fact stayed on the path even in the darkness, even in the disconnectedness of denying the truth. Consciousness of the cosmos is all around us. It envelops and caresses us. It nourishes us with truth, with love, and the interconnected-ness of the knowledge that everything is possible.

Connected consciousness leads to awakening, and, even-tually, to enlightenment. Animals are embodied enlightened souls that sign up for missions, sometimes multiple missions, to support our human spiritual journey back to enlightenment, to the Light, and the All. They are assigned mission reports and will do whatever it takes to complete their mission, their reason for embodiment. They will manifest disease to support the journey of the soul or souls they are assigned to help. They will take on abuse and neglect in the process of waking up their wards. They freely accept this mission. They remain awakened. They remain connected to truth.

Shortly after the second awakening, my soul was assigned a special unique task to read the missions of the furry ones that came into my practice. I studied multiple medical techniques and yet found that the reading of the 'mission report' became the pivotal shift for both pet and the human connected with it. Yet fear kept me quiet, and I would speak in clinical terms and human behavior language to convey this mission to the furry ones' ward. I did not want people to hurt me anymore. I spent years trying to fit in, and years of trying to follow the rules. Years progressed, and essential oils, crystals, and plants spoke to me. I would combine all these medical energies to support healing the human-animal bond, so the pet could continue to do his or her mission. I acquired a council of etheric souls that would guide me. All the energies would communicate, and we would decide what was best. I communicate with the pet, not his or her earth consciousness, but the consciousness of the soul embodied within the furry package. This soul report, as I call it, would give me insight into a bigger picture for the pet's journey currently and whether they needed to stay or go. I know what words their human companion needs to hear. I see the bigger picture, direction, or map of the soul's journey beyond space and time. I see the entanglement of cause and effect beyond what lies on the exam table, as I did when Hie Kie chose to transition to keep my mom in place, which kept me directed. Had my mom died when I was seventeen, I would have left my path full of anger.

My business grew. I kept as safe as I could, sticking with clinical takes on the treatment protocols, and researching why the energies gave me a direction, so I was able to explain it to those not yet awakened. I pioneered a medical modality known as Veterinary Medical Aromatherapy® just through doing what I was directed to do and then researching why those energies were chosen so I could explain them in sound science while not revealing my etheric connections. For twenty years now, I have kept quiet and I was slowly dying. I was slowly being extinguished by dulling my own light. I was playing safe and small; I was hiding. Darker and darker energies were descending upon me. I could no longer mediate the energies surrounding me, drowning me. I could not protect those I love, the earth I love, and the inhabitants I love. Finally, I could love the humans because the animals so loved them and would sign up for pain and suffering for the good of their human companion. My light was going out.

"Wake up Nancy! Wake up!" I screamed at myself. "Speak up!" I had raised three kids on my own, built a successful business, published books and videos, and had laid the foundation of standardizing the treatment of animals with essential oils safely and effectively. I had done all of that because I focused on healing the animals. I just did what I KNEW was right to heal the animals and, later, the human-animal bond, the entangled energy of companionship, the way the energy of one system, humans, affects the other system. Yet I was fading into the darkness, tired, and on a lonely mission; forsaken, I thought.

I asked for help. I asked to leave to go home. I asked to be done, just like the two-year old flat-lining on the table; did I really need to stay? My entire family, mother, brother, and then father committed suicide. Could I just put out my own light? Was it mine to put out? No, the answer is NO! This light in us is part of a bigger plan, a plan of interconnections beyond our scope of understanding. In terms of quantum physics, it is the string theory of string theory. Consciousness is outside of us. It is an entangled web of light in the All and is known as the zero-point field in quantum mechanics.

In the zero-point field, all energy is in a state of unlimited potential. The atom is in a state of infinite possibilities, outside of time and space that are just constructs of a human understanding of reality. Our language cannot fully explain it. Mathematics is the better language right now to describe the ever-revealed quantum universe. In my journey back to the Light, I have found only one universal truth: there is truth in all things and nothing is Truth. Our human language is inadequate to explain all Truth. Our humanness can lead to darkness or light. We live in a duality that only exists in our perception of the world, but the truth is that there is no duality, only Oneness, beauty, connectedness and love. We come from the one, and, to have a human journey, we take on three-dimensional form and duality. If we notice the beauty of these words on the page or the resonance of them, the song they sing to us, the picture of truth they reveal to us, that is the One. When we make the words mean this or that, we are in dualism. Instead, when we feel them as one piece of a larger picture of truth, that is the taste of oneness. In that moment, we are connected with the beauty of the All. We can choose to make things mean something, or we can choose to sit in the beauty of the experience.

"Do you remember who I am?" whispered the Seraph. I saw him, his connections, his mission beyond our construct of time and space. I saw him in the Light, the All, the interconnections of the cosmos. I experienced him. No meaning or language really could describe him. He brought energies or waveforms to humans again to support his larger mission and to support human kind to raise their consciousness and to wake up! He had held me that day so many years ago, as I chose to re-embody that little two-year olds' body. He had directed me. Now he was here to re-energize me. He was here to support me, and all humans who chose to do so, with new wavelengths of energy, with updated software as the Seraphim Blueprint founder, Ruth Rendely, says.

Level One of the Seraphim Blueprint course initiated an energy I had never felt on Earth before; only in the loving arms of my angelic siblings did I ever feel such love and strength of energy. I could use this to heal the animals and myself. I signed up for the festival that was synchronistically timed to be in town the next weekend. Ask and ye shall receive. The answers are always there if you just listen. Be present and listen, feel, see, and know. In the quiet spaces between the construct of the here and now and the chaos of duality, black or white, right or wrong, yes or no, lives the answer, the truth.

At the festival, in Las Vegas 2017, I met embodied souls of incredible energy and truth. They are humble souls who stand for truth. Exposure to the Seraphim Blueprint is like getting the map of how to connect to the zero-point field. It is there, in the field, where the ultimate potential lives. The field is the All. There in the All is the ultimate in Love. The Seraph is generous and is laying out a blueprint for mankind's elevation in consciousness. The Seraph's plan is bigger than we can currently comprehend, so he is laying it out in a methodical way and bringing it forth in human terms of beauty and respect. These are ancient souls that will honor the holiness of the task of raising consciousness in a world currently full of "Haters." The age of Love must emerge victorious.

Those days in the woods with my teacher Hie Kie involved elevating my consciousness, my coming to love the wholeness of the planet Earth, Gaia, her soul, and all those souls who inhabit her. The Seraph whispered in my ear, "Remember who you are! You are your truth, share your truth, and speak up. Voice the truth; heal the animals, all the animals including humans." It is my time to be fully awakened and speak truth. No more hiding behind intellectual truth. It is my time, and, people this is bigger than us! All I have to say to all of you is WAKE UP! WAKE UP NOW!

* * *

Nancy Brandt, DVM, has studied human behavior and aromatherapy to assist the collective consciousness of pets and their guardians. In 1999 she founded the Natural Care Institute, a holistic veterinary practice. She is also the founder of the Veterinary Medical Aromatherapy Association. In 2017 she founded the UnBound Center for Animal Wellness. Nancy is a mother, grandmother and guardian to many.

Good Grief

Dear Mom,

I can't believe it has been twenty-four years since you suddenly died. July 14, 1992 will forever be etched in my mind and heart. Last night, I had a dream that not only revealed the powerful effect of that trauma on me, but also gave me a deep sense of hope.

The dream took place in a dark parking garage. After climbing into the back seat of a car, I realized that the driver had a bomb. Hurling myself to the other end of the seat, I pushed open the door and tumbled out just before the car exploded. Rolled into a ball in a corner and shaking, I heard myself say, "I thought it would kill me." Waking up, I understood that "it" was your death; then I heard the words, "I am not ready to die."

I was not ready to die, even though my heart broke at the news of your death. In fact, recently I have had a remarkable healing from the pain of your passing, and I want to take a few moments to tell you this story.

You knew, when I turned forty in April of 1992, how thrilled Fred and I were to have seven-year old Sara, but you knew also how we longed for a second child. In June of that year, I became pregnant but lost the baby within the month.

In July I was sufficiently recovered for my doctors to give me the "go ahead" for our already-planned trip to Spain, where Fred and I had met and had been making an annual journey.

Strangely, before every international flight, I experienced a nightmare; fortunately, each trip went smoothly. But in 1992 I had no nightmare and was curious what that might indicate. Dismissing my thought as superstition, I resolved to have a fun vacation.

Even before arriving at Logan Airport in Boston, we had problems which continued every step of the journey. Most were small issues—forgotten items, grape juice spilled on beige carpet, laundry mishaps. Thinking of how you often handled situations, I laughed them off and reassured myself everything would be fine.

After visiting with friends in western Spain, we travelled to the southeast coast where we had rented an apartment. One evening Sara became ill. She often had fevers, but that night her body turned stone cold. A trip to the emergency room revealed an ear infection requiring medication.

Two days later, I experienced intense abdominal pain. As the doctors at home had warned me that the miscarriage might have complications, we returned to the hospital to discover that I had a urinary tract infection. Another prescription.

A few days later, with the doctor's permission, I decided to go swimming to release the stress. When I returned, can you imagine how baffled I was when little Sara asked, "Mommy, why is your face green?" A call to the hospital revealed an interaction between the pool water and the medications. Was there no end to this?

On July 14, I woke with an intense desire to call you, but in 1992 no one had cell phones. I chastised myself for being a "baby." All I really wanted was to hear your voice, but I let the possibility go and continued with my morning routines.

At one o'clock, someone knocked on our door with a telegram from Charlie, asking that I call. Panicked, I wondered why my brother wanted to talk. I raced to the only available public phone and then heard my brother's broken voice tell me you had died of a heart attack earlier that day.

NO! NO! NO! That was all I could scream the entire way back to our apartment.

Knowing I couldn't let Sara see me so distraught, I immediately did what I had watched you do for forty years. I buried every emotion inside me and calmly shared the news. Of course, I cried, but I did not allow anyone to see how broken my heart was.

Suddenly, I understood why I had wanted to call you that morning. After a heart attack the prior evening, you had been taken to the hospital. The doctors had assured Charlie you would be fine. However, you had been a widow for fourteen years and were ready to leave this life. As I calculated the six-hour time difference between Spain and Ohio, I realized that you had been lying in your hospital bed thinking of me and saying good-bye at the same time I had wanted to call you.

That night, you came to me in a comforting dream. Although you always dressed nicely and drove a practical car, in the dream you were driving a red convertible with the top down and were wearing very elegant boots. With your usual good cheer, you drove off, waving and repeating, "I love you all very much!"

After flying directly to Cleveland, we had a lovely memorial service. Before the reception, I was not sure I could bear to greet all your friends and our relatives. However, the first person in line exclaimed with joy, "Your mom would have loved this day!" It was true—you always loved a party, and this one was in your honor. As though you were standing next to me, I felt capable of speaking with everyone.

When we returned home, I busied myself with life—family, teaching, and projects. In September I became pregnant again, only to lose the baby in November. As I sat on the hospital bed after the D&C, I looked at all the sympathy cards people had sent after your death. Although I could not bear to acknowledge it, grief had stolen my heart.

Sixteen months after your death, how I wished you could have been with me for the birth of Alex. I knew you had helped with that miracle. Now with two children, I was very busy. Family life was also the perfect way to avoid dealing with my sorrow. Four years later, however, I ended up in the hospital with pneumonia and a fractured back. Life had forced me to stop.

As I recovered, I found myself very drawn to angels. Although I had gone to Sunday school, the only angels I knew about were the ones in the Christmas carols that I loved to sing. Nonetheless, my interest was unrelenting; I began reading and learning.

Sara and I had the remarkable opportunity of spending a weekend studying with Dr. Doreen Virtue, well-known angel expert, during one of her few visits to the East Coast. I then took classes that prepared me to do angel readings and therapeutic sessions for others. With each training, I felt more supported and loved; this allowed my heart to begin healing.

From 2004 until 2007, I worked with several intuitives who told me I would write a book. As I had never considered this, I was surprised and did not know where to start. In 2008 I unexpectedly received an email about an online writing course taught by Dr. Gay Hendricks, psychologist and author of thirty-five books. Feeling guided to study, I took the first class.

The assignment was to select a project. I had no idea what to write. That morning, just before meditating, I asked the angels. The immediate answer was, "Write letters to your mother." I knew I could do that. After all, I had written weekly letters to you from the time I left for college until your death.

For the next eight years, I poured my heart into letters, writing as though you were only miles, not dimensions away. For the first time since 1992, I allowed myself to cry. I had been afraid to start, fearing the tsunami of tears would never end. However, I discovered that tears are a healing force when allowed to flow.

The entire project was like a thousand-piece jigsaw puzzle. Completing the puzzle would bring closure to your death, but I did not have a picture on the box top to guide me. I wrote and wrote, hoping each piece would interlock with the others. Every letter was guided by angels. Often, I woke in the middle of the night to write. Sometimes a dream would reveal a missing memory or help me understand one of the many emotions that accompany grief.

People asked how I was progressing, but I knew the book had its own timeline. My hope was that, somehow, I would know when I had finished. On occasion a poem would come to me, such as this one:

The Greatest Mentor

Grief, grief
GRIEF
Buried deep within

Grief, grief
GRIEF
Too painful to approach

Grief, grief
GRIEF
Burning in my soul

I cannot bear to look
The wounds are so profound
Descending into feelings
Too horrific to consider

In my cavernous soul
A flame has just appeared
A tiny spark of light
To illumine the dark road

To light the hellish journey
That beckons to my heart
To reclaim the myriad pieces
From their shattering, long ago

A million shards of glass
From that broken heart
Polished through the years
By unshed tears of love

Is it finally safe?
To descend the ladder now
Into that darkened cavern
Where wounded Helens lie?

If I take this journey
Will I re-emerge
Blackened from the ashes
Or illumined by the love?

Grieving, grieving
Grieving
I let the tears run free

Grieving, grieving
Grieving
The flame begins to glow

Grieving, grieving
Grieving
I comfort my own soul

Loved ones won't return
My heart will always ache
But the searing pain
Lessens its tight grip

The journey into dark
Though frightening at the start
Begins to teach the lessons
That only death can show

The lesson of forgiveness
For imperfect human love
The lesson of compassion
For a journey we all share

Death is not the enemy
It is the greatest mentor
Teaching us to love
Our broken suffering souls

On May 8, 2016, I sat down to write a letter and to cry. When I reread the words, I knew the project was complete. The ending of that letter was different. There was a sense of peace in my heart. How appropriate because it was Mother's Day. I felt such joy that morning!

In late June, we went back to Spain, our first trip to the Mediterranean Coast since that fateful summer of 1992. It was as though a circle was being completed. As I meditated one morning shortly after arriving, I was immediately guided to write the prologue and epilogue for my book of letters.

Just before leaving for Spain, I unexpectedly lost a tooth. The dentist assured me I would be able to have an implant, so the loss would not be noticeable. Consultation with a specialist indicated I needed a bone graft first and that I would have to use steroids after the surgery.

Unfortunately, I received a Lyme tick-bite in August;

a great deal of medication was required to resolve the infection. I could not use the steroids until I finished the Lyme protocol, so my surgery was postponed until the end of January 2017.

As I was preparing for the procedure, I understood that subconscious fears were surfacing to be healed. The angels guided me to work with Dr. Sandi Radomski, holistic psychotherapist and creator of the mind body technique "Ask and Receive."

Mom, Dr. Radomski helped me understand that I was still repressing the trauma of Uncle Stan's unsuccessful surgery and death, coupled with losing you and Dad unexpectedly—despite extensive care from doctors.

A few days before my oral procedure, I woke filled with anxiety. I asked the angels to please help me. While in the shower, I had a vision of sitting on the hospital bed after my D&C in November of 1992 and responding to the sympathy cards for your death. My subconscious was offering me an opportunity to heal that painful memory and all the grief connected to it.

Working again with Dr. Radomski, I could release the trauma and heal my relationship with you, Mom. I saw our two hearts connected by a shining bridge of yellow light. I had held on to the grief because it kept me connected with you, but I no longer need that sadness. Now you are anchored in my heart, and we are bonded through joy. I felt a deep sense of peace both prior to and after the dental surgery.

Mom, I have missed you every day. I thought your death would kill me; instead, it has made me stronger. Knowing that you and the angels were near, I could find the courage to examine not only my grief but also every emotion that comes with loss.

It was a daunting task to face each feeling I had buried deeply in my soul; anger was the hardest. For many years, I had felt abandoned since you left without warning. As I wrote, I understood that you not only cherished me but also wanted to give me the greatest gift possible—freedom. Since you never wanted me to take care of you, you kept your health concerns private.

Mom, I always appreciated how you supported me and my dreams as well as my family without being controlling or intrusive. Your gifts have been unending. I have no doubt you encouraged me to study angels so they could help me reconnect with you. I have learned a tremendous amount about grief. I hope that I can now help others who deal with the searing pain of loss.

Thank you for teaching me how to love and laugh, how to guide Sara and Alex, and how to find the gift in each new challenge. I love you and know you are always in my heart.

Love,
Helen

* * *

Helen Fernald has worked with angels for many years, and after completing all six levels of Seraphim Blueprint, she is even more passionate about helping others connect with their angelic support. Helen's angels continue to guide her career as a published author, speaker, teacher and channel. She resides in Wolfeboro, New Hampshire.

My Day as Rama

While quietly lying in bed, half asleep-half awake, and thinking about getting up, an image appeared in my mind of a beautiful young girl, but not anyone I knew. I wondered why the image was there because it wasn't something that I'd been thinking about and it wasn't like a shifting dream. So I decided to do a little experiment. In my mind, I embraced the figure of this girl and imagined our energies merging as I did some Tantric deep breathing techniques that I'd learned many years earlier. This wasn't a sexual encounter; it was more just an experiment to see if the energies could be merged and to see if there was anything more to this experience than just an imaginary figure.

I was quite surprised that the energies began to merge as I did the breathing technique. As I continued, both energies increased and began to spiral around each other, ascending higher, and gathering more brilliant opalescent light and energy. As we went higher, the bliss, the energy, and the light continued to increase. I've had a similar experience before, but in that one, I got dropped off at some intermediate level as the masculine and feminine energies, or Shiva and Shakti, continued spiraling up to ever greater and more blissful levels which I was not able to sustain.

So I naturally expected this time that, at some point, I would get dropped off, and energy would continue on by itself; however, that didn't happen. This time, as the energy continued to rise and spiral higher, I stayed with it. In fact, the energy just got stronger, more blissful, brighter, and more ecstatic. It was becoming somewhat overwhelming. I kept wondering, how can this be, how can I continue to go up with this, and, because it was all so incredible, what could I have possibly done to deserve this? As I rose higher, the ecstasy and the bliss were so much more intense than anything I'd ever experienced, that I almost felt like I was crying because of it.

Also, it soon became apparent that this female figure was not just any ordinary girl, nor just a figment of my imagination. Rather, it became obvious that this was a form of Mother Divine, the feminine aspect of God. She had a hold of my left arm and she was lifting me up and up and making this whole experience possible. That's why I didn't get dropped off at a much lower level: she was holding on to me.

As we continued to ascend, the energy continued to increase. Finally, we reached a beautiful heavenly realm, and I noticed that, although Mother Divine was still holding me by the arm, she was now interacting with different divine beings who would come up to her with various questions and requests related to their duties on that level. She was conducting the administration of all those divine levels as she continued to raise the energy in my system.

Then I noticed that, since we were up in this celestial or heavenly world, we weren't physically going any higher. However, the energy was continuing to rise within my body and increasing in intensity. Earlier, we were ascending levels, and each level was more intense than the previous one, but now that we'd reached the highest level, she began to raise the energy in my body. As it started moving up through my feet and legs and rising through the rest of my body, it took on a unique quality, and soon it was apparent that this was the energy of Lord Ram, or Rama the celestial ruler. In the Vedic tradition of India, Rama is an incarnation or aspect of God that occasionally incarnates on Earth to restore natural law and order.

As this energy of Ram continued to rise in my system, Mother Divine occasionally glanced at me to check its progress, and then she resumed her duties of dealing with the celestial residents who came for instructions. Once the energy had almost filled my entire body, Mother Divine dismissed all the other celestial residents, ending her session of instructing them and, instead, putting all her attention on me. As she watched, the energy filled me from my toes to my head, but then she continued to bring in the energy so that it went just a hair higher than her own. Now I know this may sound crazy, but it seemed that she wanted her manifestation of Rama to be just a hair taller than she was because she could not be devoted to anyone less than, or even just equal to herself in energy and stature. So she had to make me equal, at least energetically, to her and maybe even just a touch more, and at that point, the process was complete. Then she turned and, facing me, she radiated amazing love and devotion to the Rama she had created through my system.

The strange thing was that even though I was feeling more bliss in energy and ecstasy than I have ever experienced in my entire life, there was another part of me that was still just me. Just the same witness that had experienced being John Chandler earlier was now experiencing being Rama or, at least, the manifestation of Ram energy in a physical form. This was a little confusing because I was experiencing this incredible energy, light, and bliss along with the amazing love and devotion of Mother Divine towards the new Ram she had created, while, at the same time, I was experiencing just being the same witness that I've always been.

Then I had the thought that this was all great and wonderful, but I'm married, and what do I do about my wife? Then Mother Divine directed my attention to some celestial palace where my wife was being hosted as a royal guest. My wife just said, "I'm doing great honey. You just do whatever Mother Divine wants you to." Next I said, "I have earthly children; who is going to take care of them?" Mother directed my attention to my children who were also up in the heavenly region. They were running around having a great time exploring all the different areas of heaven, and they also said, "Don't worry about us, Dad, we're doing great and having a wonderful time. Just do whatever Mother wants you to." So it seemed that everyone else was quite fine with this whole development, but, ironically, I questioned why nobody asked me whether I was fine with it. I was the only one who didn't seem to have anything to say about it, even though I was the focal point of the whole experience.

As I pondered about this experience, I noticed that a new energy began to rise along the left side of my body, starting in my feet and then rising up my leg and up. This was between me and Mother Divine, and then it began to emerge and take shape and form out of the left side of my body. As it took form, I became aware that this was the energy of

Lord Hanuman manifesting. I had the thought that in the Vedic literature, Hanuman is portrayed as a great devoté of Rama. I thought that was interesting; however, my impression now is that Hanuman is either an expression of, or a manifestation of some aspect of the Rama energy, or, more likely, it is a result of the union of the energies of Mother Divine and Rama. Anyway, this expression of Hanuman had white fur. I don't know why it was white, and I don't know why the union of Mother Divine's and Rama's energies might manifest as Hanuman who is the king of the monkeys in Indian mythology. He is described as extremely strong and powerful, and he was instrumental in winning some of the legendary battles with the forces of darkness in the epic tale of the Ramayana. Once Hanuman's form became solid enough, he detached from my body and went off to do whatever he was supposed to do.

Next, Mother Divine informed me that now it was time for me to perform my duties. So she took me by the arm and led me to a giant chair where I sat down. Then her servants brought up some resident of the heavenly realm, who had either broken a law or done something wrong, and it was now my job to judge him and order the appropriate punishment. As I looked at this person, I could see on his left side that there were light brown and crusty ropes that were wrapped around his subtle body, ropes which covered about 20 to 30% of his being. It was obvious that these cords were the ignorance, or sin, or mistakes that he had made. As I looked at this person, I noticed that whenever my mind switched to thinking about judging him, the incredible energy, bliss, and light that were still flowing up through my body would stop, and, worse yet, when I thought about punishing him, the energy would recede. So I stopped the thoughts of judgment or punishment. I turned to Mother Divine and said, "I can't do this. This energy that I'm experiencing is much too precious and valuable, and any time I start to think about judging or punishing it stops or decreases. I am not willing to lose that energy, so you'll just have to find someone else to do any punishment that might be necessary." But everyone just continued to look at me expectantly and waited to see what I would do.

So I looked back at this person and decided that I was going to change my role. I said that I was redefining my role of increasing the light energy, love and bliss everywhere I could in creation. I would leave punishment and karma up to the Lords of Karma. Punishment was not going to be part of my responsibility. Then, as I put my attention on this person, who was kneeling and trembling with terrible fear because here he was facing the new Rama and he was certain that he was going to be sent to hell for whatever he had done. However, instead of doing that, I directed the flow of energy that was coming up through me with light, bliss and love, to flow out of me instead and towards him. What happened next was truly amazing to watch. The energy just blasted and obliterated all those cords of ignorance and sin that had been wrapped around the left side of his body, and, instantly, he was transformed from a less than normal celestial resident to a completely purified and perfected divine being. He was so stunned and shocked at this outcome, that he just fell down and said, "Thank you Lord. Thank you, thank you, thank you." I turned to Mother Divine and said, "I'm sorry; that's all I can do. I'm not willing to stop or interrupt the flow of this light, bliss and energy."

Apparently, word gets around up there very fast, almost instantly; so then another being came up to be judged. However, as I looked at this one, I clearly saw that he was a rakshasa, or demon, cleverly disguised as a celestial resident. His body was covered by seventy to eighty percent of this same brown crusty cord, starting again from his left side and covering most of him, but I could see there was still a small area that wasn't covered. I could feel his thoughts and I noticed that he had come with the intention of discrediting me and proving that what people were saying about how I handled the previous person could not possibly be true. Also, he wanted to kill me.

This realization elicited a wave of fear in me, and I thought that I should protect myself, but as soon as I felt that fear and had that thought, I noticed again that this light, energy, bliss, and love, which was flowing through me, stopped and began to recede. I couldn't allow that, so I immediately stopped those thoughts, telling myself that this energy was just too precious, and I was not going to think in terms of fear, even if it meant that he attacked me and killed me. So then, I looked at him and thought, well, what should I do with him now? Okay, I have redefined my role as one of just purifying all of creation as much as possible, and spreading this light, love, bliss and energy everywhere I can. So I directed that flow of energy to him, and the same thing happened as before, even though he was covered with cording up to seventy or eighty percent. It was all instantly obliterated, and he was transformed from a demon, disguised as a celestial resident, to a fully purified and perfected divine being. He was so shocked and stunned that this had happened, and so grateful that he fell on his knees and, bowing down, said, "thank you Lord, thank you."

At this point I looked up I saw that my teachers, Maharishi and Guru Dev[1], appear in the sky. They looked so big, beautiful, magnificent and unbounded that I pointed to them and said, "I want to be like them." Mother Divine turned to me and had a fit. She said, "After I've elevated you to this level, you want to be like them?" And with that she turned and gathered up all of heaven, all the light, bliss and energy, and she moved into the distance, and all I could see was her back as she left. (Apparently, my wanting to be like two life-long celibates was not what she'd had in mind for me as her consort). After she left, all the extreme energy and bliss were gone, and I was left floating in a soft bluish-white light of unbounded space. But since I wasn't there through my own perfection, or my own energy, I began to sink, and as I sank deeper and deeper, I did not sink down into my previous American body, but into the body of a poor peasant woodcutter in the jungles of India.

I was totally shocked. What is this? First I get elevated to be Rama, King of heaven, and now because I accidentally offended Mother Divine by wanting to be someone that I thought was great and wonderful like Maharishi and Guru Dev, now I'm cast down and into the body of a poor starving peasant in India. That was just too much, so I thought, alright, if I'm going to sink this far, then I'm going to continue sinking all the way. So I sat down and started meditating.

As I meditated, I began to sink deeper into creation, and as I sank into some of the deepest levels, I noticed that another, different, energy was coming up into my body. Soon

---

[1] Maharishi Mahesh Yogi (1918 – 2008) and "Guru Dev" is Shankaracharya Swami Brahmananda Saraswati (1868 – 1953)

I recognized this energy as being the energy of Lord Shiva, another aspect of God. Finally, I sank to the deepest level of creation and entered Shiva's realm just at the level of the first emergence of the finest level of creation out of the transcendent. I floated in his domain, and there was Shiva sitting in meditation, completely absorbed in the transcendent, which is what I would have expected.

Next I noticed that it was somewhat cool down there. At first I didn't know why it would be cool, but as I thought about it, it occurred to me that Shiva is the expression of the transcendent, which is state of least excitation, so this must be a realm that is closest to absolute zero. That made sense, but it wasn't bitter cold. It was just refreshingly cool. It was also softly lit there, like a night sky with a bright moon. There was nobody else there, just me and Shiva. So I thought, all right, I'm going to stay here where it's pure, eternal, non-changing, and not subject to the whims and moods of women and goddesses who can raise you to heaven, or send you to what I'm sure would've felt like hell on earth.

As I sat there, I noticed that there really wasn't much to do. It was pretty boring. Shiva was doing his thing, and there was no one else to talk to. So, I thought, all right, I still have my consciousness, so I'll go back up into my own body, resume my life, and enjoy it as much as I can for as long as it lasts. I came back up into this body, but before I had a chance to open my eyes and get out of bed, Mother Divine came back. By this time, she had calmed down and she said to me, "All right, you can worship me through your wife." Then she placed a big crown on my wife's head. This crown was the shape of a big pine cone completely covered in brilliant sparkling diamonds. I thought, great, my wife gets a crown, and I just barely escaped from being a poor woodcutter in India, how is that fair?" Then Mother turned to me and she said, it's okay, you get a crown too. Then she put a similar big tall cone shaped crown covered with diamonds on my head and left.

So that was my experience of what it was like being elevated to heaven and what it might feel like to be Rama, crashing down to be a poor woodcutter in India, continuing down to stay with Shiva, and coming back to my normal body. I have no idea how any of this could be true, but when I've talked to various clear people, psychics, and pundits, they meditated on it and said that, yes, they thought it was a true experience. So I have no idea what to think of it. It was much more than a dream, but how could something so fantastic be real, except they say that all of creation is just the play of Maya in God's mind, so anything is possible. Next time, I'll think first before saying anything that might offend Mother Divine; after all, being King of Heaven and Mother Divine's consort looked like a pretty sweet deal.

* * *

John Chandler has been a TM Meditation instructor for 44 years, and since 2010 an enthusiastic student and Teacher of Seraphim Blueprint and planetary energies. He resides on the west side of Minneapolis in Excelsior, Minnesota, teaching the Divine Biosphere and Seraphim Blueprint in local groups and telephone conferencing.

A Thousand Years

"You have lived more than a thousand years."

What!? Listening to my inner angel voice, I'm still processing the almost instantaneous past-life recall that had just occurred while sitting on the beach. I should be used to this type of message, but this one really took me by surprise. Why? A black cat speaks to me like we were just sitting here having a friendly chat.

Let me start from the beginning. My daughter Faith and her husband are away on vacation and have offered me their home in Virginia Beach for a vacation of my own. I've always loved the beach, and this visit to Virginia Beach would give me the great opportunity to revisit Edgar Cayce's Association for Research and Enlightenment (ARE).

It was July 2000; I arrived on the 17th and unpacked quickly, so that I could make my appointment for a reading and a massage at ARE's Heritage Store. On the drive to the store, I thought of what questions I would have for the psychic reader at ARE's. Where do I want to go? What is best for me? And, I thought, "What would make me happy?" The angel's voice popped in, "Time to write life-lessons story books for children." I knew this wasn't my own thought, as I had not considered writing any books. This was an idea that will go on my bucket list.

Two days later, I went to the beach early in the morning with a beach chair, a journal, and a large cup of coffee. It was quiet this time of morning; there were mostly a few walkers and fishermen. I could smell the fresh air and feel a light breeze on my skin. The sun was already warm on my face, and I closed my eyes, just allowing my body to relax in the moment. As I watched the Atlantic Ocean, I was mesmerized by the sound of the waves going in and out. Just listening and connecting, I began to breathe with Gaia. Watching the ocean rise to the peak of each wave, I noticed that these waves always fell forward and, as each one receded, another wave came in toward the beach. I felt they were a message that, even though we are moving forward, we sometimes feel that we are going backwards. I couldn't help but notice that the beach had been "combed" and regraded. This was another message for me: a new slate for everyone who sits on this beach today. What a marvelous morning.

I also noticed the many birds along the shore line, chasing the waves out and then dancing back as the water came forward. I assumed they were looking for a tasty breakfast. "Yes, that's true", my angel's voice said in my head, "But do you want to know why else they are here?" I smiled, since I know the voice will tell me regardless of whether I answer "yes" or "no". Obviously, this was going to be a very special day of talking to my angels and writing their messages in my journal. The angels shared a very important morning ritual with me, the one that the beach birds do every day.

The angels asked me to close my eyes, as they wanted me to relax and remember a time that I sat on a beach, just like this, thousands of years ago. Trained as a hypnotherapist who specializes in Past-Life Therapy and Meditation, I was interested in the memory. The veil lifted, and I saw myself as a young girl, named Morganna, sitting on a rocky beach with a black cat called Magick. As Magick and Morganna sat watching the waves and the birds, I found it interesting that she took no notice of the birds. The scene seemed familiar, and I felt that I was waiting for Magick to speak. I, as Morganna, knew that she has spoken to me before to remind me of a memory or to share an adventure. Morganna sat patiently. She and I merged completely.

I noticed that Magick was looking out over the ocean. She pointed out two large dolphins to me, which were traveling south along the coast line, diving in and out of the water. Magick said, "Do you remember when we sat like this before?" Immediately, I thought of Scotland, and the beach turned into a rocky coastline. Magick and I sat, looking out over the water. I knew we were taking a break from my magical teachings with Merlin. Today's lesson was a journey through the elements to awaken our psychic senses and our ability to see, hear, sense, know, and feel. We had already studied earth, air, fire, and water. I sat patiently, while Magick began to explain the importance of respecting the water and Mother Earth. This lesson seemed to be more important than the previous ones of making predictions, seeing auras, and moving objects across the table through the power of mind alone.

"MORGANNA"—Magick said my name in a stern but loving voice. "Watch the ocean; it is our lifeline; we must take care of her. Every year, special children are born, to help Mother Earth and others, and you have been chosen for this life purpose." I was grateful for the reminder. Magick continued, "Do you have anyone that you would like to help ease their sadness, pain; or someone you just want to be happy? Go now to the water's edge, where the sand is still wet. Write their name in the sand, just above where the wave clears the beach and then just be patient." I (as Morganna) could not wait to try this. I ran to the ocean's edge.

I watched where the ocean wave stopped and picked a place to write a name. I wrote my own name in the wet sand, thinking, "I always want to be happy." Then I stood and watched the waves. The waves came in and out about four times and then, on the fifth wave, they washed over the name, erasing it in the sand, but taking it out to the ocean. I felt a difference of energy, and it was then that I understood the power of the lesson. The water released the prayer of healing for the person who is named. "Yes", Magick said, "That is right. We must take care of the ocean as it has the power to erase and clear a person of all stress. The tide comes in to take the name, and so healing and clearing the person named of any negativity and then releasing it to the ocean."

Magick joined Morganna (with me, her later self by hundreds of years) at the ocean's edge and then walked down the beach. With each paw print in the wet sand, she said the name of a person. Morganna followed. Magick explained to her that this was another way that one could help other people. "Just say a name or a prayer, for each footprint as you walk the beach," she said. The waves did their job and washed over the footprints. "One more important part of the lesson," said Magick, "is to write the name of the ocean/lake/river/water where you are doing this ritual. This is how you can help the water to heal itself." Morganna wrote the name "Atlantic Ocean". She could feel the vibrational energy change in her hand even as she wrote. It was as if hundreds of angels had just come forward to connect and support. Thinking that this would be even more powerful with a group of people who are one in consciousness, she knew that she had to share this with everyone. If everyone would just visit the ocean, or any body of water, and would take the time to do this, it would help Mother Earth.

Water is sacred. The water has power and we must honor and respect it. Magick smiled while thinking, "If only all the children of Mother Earth remembered this lesson when they grow up. Maybe the angels will help spread the word in the dreamtime of all those who could be recruited.

"Come, Morganna, it is time to go back to Merlin's hidden cave." This cave was well concealed and could only be seen by those that Merlin had chosen to do magical work. "It is time to teach you about the power and the magic of fire by giving them respect."

Suddenly, my eyes opened, and I was back at Virginia Beach. I began to write as fast as I could in my journal. I wanted to remember every word and detail of my experience. When I finished, I got up and walked to the ocean's edge. I wrote the names of my children, Christine and Faith, as well as that of my son-in-law, in the wet sand and watched the waves take them away. I wrote the words, "Atlantic Ocean", and the waves released the prayer. As I turned south, I walked, and with each step, I named my grandchildren, parents, family, and friends. Ah, so this is why the birds are here every morning. I get it. I understand now. I received other names in my thoughts, names I did not know. I realized that I was helping the bird-angels with their morning job. I just knew that each print represented a person who has prayed to their angels and asked for a healing. I loved helping with this work. I also agreed to help and support these angel-birds every time I was at the beach.

I have lived a thousand years and now wonder how many lifetimes it has been in which I have shared this message. I have always loved the beach, and in this life, I once again remember that I can do this. Everyone can do this. I think I will share this experience with all my friends and everyone I meet, and I'll write a children's book to share this story.

* * *

Sandra McGill is a retired certified hypnotherapist, who specializes in meditation and past life regressions, and has worked with angels for 25 years. She is, also, a Seraphim Blueprint Teacher, Reiki Master, and Shaman and is trained in Theta Healing, Therapeutic Touch, Munay Ki and Ama Deus.

The Rainbow Bridge Crossing

Some say when you get a dog, you just know. That's not how it was for me. When my husband Clyde went to pick up Rico, he said he knew the dog would be mine. But Rico was a *Rottweiler*. I just couldn't get past the stereotypes.

I continued resisting Rico until Clyde handed him to me at the pet store that evening. One look in to the depths of Rico's dark brown eyes while he snuggled his fuzzy snout into my arms, and my heart was gone. Those deep dark eyes held the truth of stories yet to be told and lives already lived. Somehow, I knew that, even though we'd just met. It was as if time stood still for a few clicks. Something in the back of my mind stirred, something that I wasn't sure of, yet knew was the truth: Rico was here for me.

As Rico grew, I learned to care for a Rottweiler German Shepard mix. He was a very strong-willed dog who would top out near one hundred pounds. What a dog he was: loyal, loving, protective, silly, stubborn, strong, playful, and a true guardian. We became a close-knit couple of pals who went everywhere we could together. I took him to the dog beach where he tried to learn how to swim, but mostly he just kept the other dogs away from me. We went for walks together almost every day. Those were some of our most treasured times. Our carefree days—before our son came...

When Rico was two, he was mostly well-trained, and then a miracle—I was pregnant. Our lives flipped upside down.

Two thousand and nine was a challenging time financially for everyone, and as a result, I was working reduced hours. Rico adapted to my being home, and our bond strengthened. As the baby grew, I was changing, not just physically, but emotionally, and mentally; and though I didn't know it at the time, psychically as well. My little baby was changing me in ways I didn't understand, and he wasn't even here yet.

I believe that God, the universe (choose whatever your most comfortable word may be for the recognition of the Source beyond us) was calling me to fulfill my contract or blueprint which had lain dormant for years. God was using my son as the catalyst to revive and remind me of my own commitments to fulfill here on Earth. I began to seek out the truth of who I was, why I was here, what purpose my life held, and how it fit with my son. Such catalysts rarely come without "trauma and drama" (thanks to the beautiful Roy Burns[2] for helping me learn how to create without so much pain and suffering). At this point in my life, an ugly catalyst of the past reared up, forcing me to look good and hard at myself, and think about what it would take for me to be the kind of parent that I wanted to be.

Many tears were spilled during these months of growth, and, always, my Rico was there. He would force me to be comforted by his love. Rico would lift my hand with his big snout and place it on his neck, while looking deeply into

---

[2] http://rlbempire.com/index.html

my eyes. It was as if he said, "It's alright Mama; I love you no matter what." He'd lick my tears with his big tongue until I would giggle and gently cradle his weighty head on my stomach as if to remind me, "It's not good for the babe for you to cry so much, Mama." During this difficult time of processing, Rico showed me unconditional love, and for the first time in my life, I truly felt the power of a love inexpressible. I knew beyond a doubt that Rico's love was a soul connection. After I understood such things, I referred to him as "my soul dog." I am so grateful to have experienced such a strong connection, powerful beyond words, love beyond time and space, and an immeasurable bond that, today, passes through the veil between our worlds.

In November 2009, our son was born. His coming into the world was traumatic to say the least. Having your nose and mouth suctioned due to meconium stained amniotic fluid as the first thing that happens after you come from the womb isn't exactly the sweetest welcome to this world. It left our boy scarred. Soon enough it was time for us to leave the hospital. My husband, Clyde, put some blankets in the car and drove around with Rico so that he could adjust to the baby's new smell. It worked like a charm. The moment we camehome with the baby, Rico took to him with love.

Rico became an observer of sorts. He watched the baby, Clyde, and me. He observed our interactions to relearn his place in the family. We still went for walks, sometimes with the baby, sometimes by ourselves. We went to the dog park. We would play together in the yard, and as the boy grew, Rico began to run around just to hear him giggle. He was a silly dog, and his goal in life was to make us laugh.

Then, the hard times started. Our son wasn't developing

as he should be. He couldn't eat solid food. Doctors' visits, tests, therapies, evaluations—it seemed like I was in the car more than I was home. Diagnoses came and went: Apraxia of Speech, Sensory Processing Disorder, and then finally —after years of more therapy when he went to pre-school at age three and still being non-verbal, a neurologist and a geneticist diagnosed him with Autistic Spectrum Disorder.

During this time in our lives, Rico was my saving grace. He and I would sit on the floor together and cuddle after a long day. Often, it was the shared silence with Rico that got me through those difficult years. He was just there; even though I had no time to walk him; even though I barely had time to shower and feed myself; he was still there: to rest his head on my knee; to force me to pet his neck when he knew I needed the comfort. Rico really was my best friend. I know it's the great cliché of all time: "A dog is man's best friend." But Rico lived it every single day of his life. It's who he was and why he was here: to help me understand unconditional love so that I could give it.

Time passed. I would take Andrew to his multitude of appointments after school and work while he was in school. I knew I had abilities I wasn't tapping into, but I was trying to work through my past. Slowly, I moved into a space of ease and forgiveness so that I could be more open to the gifts that lay dormant within me. I knew I needed to understand myself better so that I could access those gifts to their fullest potential.

Through all this exploration, Rico was by my side. As I learned to meditate, he would sit near me. I developed a love for Yoga, and he would lie right next to me, sometimes with his paws on the mat.

While facing challenges with my son, I also had a friend, Wendy, who stood by my side. Her mother, Lee Shook[3], had been taking the "Seraphim Blueprint" courses. As Lee is a sharing person, she began to perform healings on my son. Then, after Lee became a certified Teacher, she spoke with me about taking the class myself. I listened intently. I bought the book, *Seraphim Blueprint* by Ruth Rendely. I was intrigued, and I also felt there was truth in the book. It also felt like something that I had done before. It felt real to me. I was one of the called.

Lee and the wonderful group of healers with whom she regularly performs energy work assisted me in the hospital for my back surgery and recovery. It was amazing! I healed quickly and am still doing great.

Shortly after that experience, I took the course "Seraphim Blueprint Level I." A year later, I took "Level II" as well. After taking "Level II," I found that I had greater access to the Seraph.

I began using the energies on myself, my son, and on Rico. Rico was beginning to show signs of old age. His hips and his knees were starting to weaken. I wanted to give him what I could so I could enjoy him for as long as possible.

In June of 2014, Rico blew out one of his knees. He was seven years old and 95 pounds when it happened. One of the ligaments of his knee gave out, and on a seven-year-old dog who may only live to be eight years old…well, you don't usually do surgery. So, I asked the vet for an alternative, and we found an amazing brace that helped to heal the tear on its own. The Mutt Knee Brace[4] is a custom-made brace that

---

[3] www.seraphimconnections.com
[4] www.muttkneebrace.com

would prove, after about eight months, to give Rico back most of the mobility in his knee. He never could go for walks again, though. That year, he officially became a Senior Dog – and a little tear in my heart formed. I knew I better treasure every year left.

Another year passed by, and we noticed that he started bumping into things. He was stuck to me like glue. Whenever a delivery person came to the door, he would go crazy. He wasn't acting like himself. So there was another trip to the vet. My Rico was losing his vision. Most of it was gone. When we got home this time, I cried. Reality was hitting me. Rico was eight and he wasn't going to live forever. I didn't realize I'd have barely a year left with him. I hugged him close, and he lay on me as he did when he was a puppy. He licked my tears and gazed into my eyes. Love is all that I could see. I began talking to him since he couldn't see me very well. I told him what I was doing and where I was going. I told him when I would be back and how much I would miss him. I told him I loved him every time I left and every time I returned. I tried to make him happy in every way I knew.

Meanwhile, I knew that I needed help in developing my intuitive abilities. I was as far as I could go with meditating on my own. I couldn't go any deeper without someone showing me the way. After inquiring, I learned about Goddess I AM[5], a metaphysical store in Naples.

Goddess I AM was like a dream, like stepping into a world of safety and love. I'd never experienced any place like it before, and it's all due to the owner, Beth Brown-Rinella. Goddess I AM had a temple room. In this room, I learned to meditate more deeply than I could have imagined. I

---

[5] www.goddessiam.com

discovered my counsel. And I spoke with the Seraph. He shared with me my mission on this earthbound journey. The Seraph used a channel created by Beth to open a dialog with me and has kept it going from that day forward.

In January of 2016 we noticed that Rico seemed to be slowing down a little and he was sleeping more. We thought it was due to old age. He was starting to look more like a senior dog and less like the puppy we remembered. He still greeted us at the door. He still couldn't wait for our son to get off the bus. He was tired, though. He slept all day. He slept all night. In February 2016, I noticed his coat was getting rather dull. It started clicking for me that, maybe, something was wrong with him. He would eat, but only 3 or 4 nights a week, even if we added some tasty treats to his food.

My dad came for a visit and he was shocked. He told me Rico looked sick. It had been so gradual that it didn't hit me how skinny he'd become. We took him to the vet that week and we found a mass on his throat. It was cancer. We got the prognosis back a week later. It wasn't good. We'd already started him on some herbal treatments, but that likely wasn't going to shrink the cancer, and it had already metastasized. We opted to just wait it out for the next couple of weeks and then bring him in for the end of life treatment.

Two weeks later, I could tell the end was near. Rico couldn't go too far without breathing hard. He needed help getting up. I went to the vet and made his funeral arrangements. The thought of voluntarily ending his life broke my heart. The thought of him struggling to his own death tore my heart to shreds. I made my selections and paid for the treatment so that, on the day we needed it, I could just bring him in. I knew the end was imminent.

The next day, I called and scheduled it for Friday. It was Wednesday. I told our son that Rico was going to go to heaven on Friday and that his doctor was going to take him there. Fortunately, he didn't ask too many questions. But he did ask, "How." I told him that the vet has special privileges, and he gets to take all the animals to the rainbow bridge where the angels then carry them across to heaven. I didn't realize that this was literally the truth.

The next morning, the Seraph came to me and told me today was the day. Rico couldn't go another night. I asked if he would please be the one to take him over the rainbow bridge. The Seraph replied gently, "Of course. He has been your guardian angel incarnate. He has a special place here. It would be my honor to carry him over the rainbow bridge to wait for you."

I cried knowing that today would be our last day together until I too joined him on the other side. I knew I would live the rest of my life without my soul dog and I ached in the loneliness of that missed connection. He just wagged his tail at me and looked at me with sad eyes. I knew today was the day, and it was time to "put my big girl panties on."

I texted my husband who came right home. We made Rico's last day the best day possible. We gave him food he'd not been allowed to eat. We made a footprint in concrete that I decorated. We spoke of remembered silliness and treasured moments with Rico near. We hugged him and we kissed him. We loved him. We waited until our son got off the bus and we let him hug Rico goodbye. I loaded Rico in the car and took some goodbye pictures of us together. Then we visited the pet store where he enjoyed doggie sniffs and gourmet treats.

When we arrived with his bed, Rico seemed confused, but he loved the vet's office. I took him back to the designated room. He went right to his bed and lay down. I petted him lightly and told him what a good boy he was.

They administered the first shot which made him relax. He looked around a little, and then he rested his head on his bed. Finally, I could hear him breathe. The vet and I looked and each other, "He wouldn't have made it another night; it's good that you brought him. Tell me when you're ready. It won't hurt him." So, I put my face next to Rico's and I asked the Seraph for strength and ease for transition. I told Rico he was the best dog ever, and that I loved him so, so much. I told him he wouldn't be in pain anymore and that I would treasure our time together until I could see him again. I stayed with my head right next to his. I kissed his nose and I gazed into his eyes. I nodded my head, and the vet administered the next shot. I just kept telling Rico how much I loved him and what an amazing dog he was.

Suddenly, an image appeared in my mind of a majestic, light-filled angel, tall and mighty, and he was gently holding my Rico in his arms. So lovingly, he looked at me, then he turned to the Rainbow Bridge in the background. The grass was electric green, and the bridge was literally rainbow-light-filled iridescence. It went up and over a vastness so wide that I couldn't see the end. There was a white light surrounding the bridge in all its beauty, and I cried out in pain as the Seraph floated out of view. Rico. Was. Gone.

I was back in the room and the vet looked at me strangely. She told me his heart was still beating. I said, "His soul is gone, he's crossed over." She listened, and a few beats later, his heart stopped. They left me with his body.

I was bewildered. I knew his soul was on the other side. I'd seen it go, but I did not want to leave his body. If I left him, he would really be gone. My guardian angel, my soul dog was truly gone. The one who taught me what unconditional love meant was gone. I lay down on his big body and held him, but soon his body grew cold, and I knew that it was time for me to leave. I felt my guardian angels tell me, "He's not there; it is time for you to go."

The Seraph asked me to share this story because so many ask what happens when their pets cross the Rainbow Bridge. Our pets are beloved creatures who return to God's side when their time on earth is done. They await our arrival back Home. Until our souls meet again, they watch over us. May this bring you comfort.

After the death of a loved one, we realize that life does go on. And my life has. I have adjusted to Rico's absence. I still hear his nails clicking on the floor tile. I hear his bark outside. I know that he watches over me. Perhaps in those moments he has found a way to come through the veil to remind me that he misses me too.

I have learned that Seraphim Blueprint can be applied to anything and everything: my health and work; my son being bullied in school. But, the most powerful event by far has been watching the Seraph gently carry the soul of my Rico over the Rainbow Bridge. It was a gift I did not have the ability to see until he gave it to me. It was a gift because he allowed me to see a tiny piece of heaven from my physical world. It was a gift because I know in my heart that my Rico is waiting for me to join him on the other side. It was a gift of a magnitude that stuns me with its profound meaning.

It is my hope that you find comfort in knowing that,

should you choose, the Seraph can and will work miracles in your life. Allow yourself to see these miracles, small and large. *YOU* are powerful and magnificent enough to experience them yourself. We all have this ability, if only we would allow ourselves to experience such gifts.

As my Counsel says to me, I say to you, "Go now surrounded in peace, love, and light."

* * *

Mary Hernandez has been a Seraphim Blueprint practitioner since 2015. She is a Naples resident, and loves year-round sunshine. She designs websites and is happily married, and with her husband supports their son's love of martial arts. She volunteers at her son's school; advocates for Autism Awareness, loves Yoga, and is rejuvenated at the beach.

2020 Seraphic Prize

In the autumn of 2020, the second Seraphic Prize will be awarded to members of the general public who compose the best spiritual short story (fictional account), or non-fiction account, with the optional mention of angels, or Seraphim. Seraphim Alliance will then publish a collection of up to fifteen stories in a volume to be published in 2021.

Individual entries are limited to 3,333 words, which is a little more than thirteen pages, of 250 words per page.

- Seraphic Prize Awards to be announced at the Triennial Seraphim Blueprint Festivals. The 2020 Seraphic Prize will be announced at the Tokyo Festival to be held in the autumn of that year.
- First prize is $1,000, plus publication
- Second prize is $500, plus publication
- Third-place prize is to be shared by thirteen authors whose work will appear in the volume to be published in 2021.
- Prize will be announced on the final day of the Festival
- Please send enquiries and entries to Ruth Rendely— ruth.rendely@seraphimblueprint.org
- All entries must be received by midnight on May 30th, 2020.

What is Seraphim Blueprint?

Thirteen thousand years ago a group of high angels called Seraphim created a cosmology that humanity could use for its 'well-being and evolution'. Atlantean priests first cognized this system. Then the early Hebrews re-cognized these energies and created the Kabbalah. In modern times the energies resurfaced in 1994 when one of the original Seraphim contacted Ruth Rendely, a meditation instructor.

The Seraphim Blueprint is a cosmological collection of energies that are permanently stored in the ethers. The Seraphim that created this system chose to give out these energies in a specific sequence that harmoniously integrates with our nervous systems.

The system includes eleven major energies that synergistically interact to enhance our life-force energy and well-being. Each major energy has its own purpose and distinct quality that together provides a unique evolutionary pathway for Self-Realization.

The energies are safe and intelligent and are pre-programmed to ideally adapt to our unique life situation and physical condition. They work on all levels of our physical, emotional, mental and spiritual bodies.

Worldwide Courses

The Seraphim Blueprint training is now available on four continents including North America, Europe, Asia and Australia. To find a Teacher in your location, please go to www.seraphimblueprint.org. The Seraphim Blueprint Levels are taken in sequence, starting with Seraphim Healing. These angelic initiations are facilitated in one or two-day workshops, either by a Teacher who is personally present, or long distance via conference calls, or through the Internet. Even if you live in a remote rural area, you will be able to receive these energies worldwide if you have access to these forms of communication. Currently, Ruth Rendely and some eighty teachers facilitate these workshops. To find out more about the courses available to you and the fees involved, please contact individual Teachers noted on the website www.seraphimblueprint.org.